Is free speech racist?

Debating Race series

David Theo Goldberg, *Are we all postracial yet?*
Ghassan Hage, *Is racism an environmental threat?*
Jonathan Marks, *Is science racist?*
Laurie Cooper Stoll, *Should schools be colorblind?*
Gavan Titley, *Is free speech racist?*
Alford A. Young, Jr., *Are Black men doomed?*

Is free speech racist?

GAVAN TITLEY

polity

The right of Gavan Titley to be identified as Author of this Work has been asserted in accordance with the UK Copyright, Designs and Patents Act 1988.

First published in 2020 by Polity Press

Reprinted 2020

Polity Press
65 Bridge Street
Cambridge CB2 1UR, UK

Polity Press
101 Station Landing
Suite 300
Medford, MA 02155, USA

ISBN-13: 978-1-5095-3615-3
ISBN-13: 978-1-5095-3616-0(pb)

A catalogue record for this book is available from the British Library.

Library of Congress Cataloging-in-Publication Data

Names: Titley, Gavan, author.
Title: Is free speech racist? / Gavan Titley.
Description: Cambridge, UK ; Medford, MA : Polity, 2020. | Series: Debating race series | Includes bibliographical references and index. | Summary: "Freedom of speech should not be used to give dangerous falsehoods a veneer of truth"-- Provided by publisher.
Identifiers: LCCN 2020007622 (print) | LCCN 2020007623 (ebook) | ISBN 9781509536153 (hardback) | ISBN 9781509536160 (paperback) | ISBN 9781509536177 (epub)
Subjects: LCSH: Freedom of speech--Social aspects. | Racism in language. | Hate speech.
Classification: LCC JC591 .T57 2020 (print) | LCC JC591 (ebook) | DDC 323.44/3--dc23
LC record available at https://lccn.loc.gov/2020007622
LC ebook record available at https://lccn.loc.gov/2020007623

Typeset in 11 on 15pt Adobe Garamond Pro
by Fakenham Prepress Solutions, Fakenham, Norfolk NR21 8NL
Printed and bound in the United States by LSC Communications

The publisher has used its best endeavours to ensure that the URLs for external websites referred to in this book are correct and active at the time of going to press. However, the publisher has no responsibility for the websites and can make no guarantee that a site will remain live or that the content is or will remain appropriate.

Every effort has been made to trace all copyright holders, but if any have been overlooked the publisher will be pleased to include any necessary credits in any subsequent reprint or edition.

For further information on Polity, visit our website: politybooks.com

For Jonas-Liam Titley

CONTENTS

Acknowledgements   viii

1 Debating racism, disputing speech   1

2 Closure: who decides what is racist?   26

3 Culture: who values free speech?   62

4 Capture: what is free speech being claimed for?   98

Afterword: so, is free speech racist?   133

Notes   138
References   140
Index   153

At Polity thanks to Jonathan Skerrett for his thoughtful and incisive editing, and to Karina Jákupsdóttir for her patience and advice. Thanks also to the manuscript reviewers for hugely useful feedback. The issues brought together in this short book are expansive and complex, and so the advice of friends on how best to approach them is more than usually appreciated. I'm grateful to Mohammed Abdi, Colm O'Cinneide, Michael Cronin, Léo Custódio, Alana Lentin and Evan Smith for clarifying conversations, and David Hesmondhalgh, Nick Riemer, Lisa Tilley and Sivamohan Valluvan for their insightful commentary on various drafts. This book is dedicated to Jonas-Liam Titley, who helped me think through many of these arguments.

ONE

Debating racism, disputing speech

Beyond the clichés of free speech crisis

The question of free speech is never far from the headlines, and in these headlines it is frequently declared to be in crisis. That these dramatic headlines proliferate in societies increasingly marked by abundant communication is curious, but this is only part of the puzzle for this book. More curious is why controversies hingeing on 'what can be said' about particular political, cultural and social issues feature so centrally in free speech crises, over and above, for example, the powerful, material and governmental threats to expression increasingly witnessed in societies marked by political surveillance and authoritarian attitudes to the press. The aim of this book is to explore why racism, in particular, has become so disproportionately integrated into these intense debates about the status and remit of freedom of speech, debates that are conducted in societies characterized not only by endless speech, but by a dominant if intensely disputed sense that racism is largely a problem that

1

has been overcome. This thorny relation between the meaning and scope of free speech, and the meaning and salience of racism, produces an apparent contradiction. In the public imagination, free speech is celebrated as a fundamental freedom, central to modern emancipation, self-expression and democratic vitality. In contemporary western societies, it has also become fundamental to an insistent, many-stranded politics that is reshaping how racism is expressed and legitimized in public culture.

'Racism' and 'free speech' are complex and disputed keywords. Often, when these keywords are invoked together, it is because racism produces questions about the limits of permissible speech. Racist discourse can and regularly does enjoy legal protection as an exercise in freedom of expression. Consequently, academic discussions of the regulation of speech often address the political and legal dimensions of this protection, and the question of if and when racist expression constitutes incitement to hatred or hate speech, and thus qualifies as a subject of restriction, censure or prosecution. In his survey of post-war legal regulation of fascist propaganda, and subsequently anti-immigrant political rhetoric and 'hate speech', Erich Bleich considers this a key dilemma for post-war European liberal democracies: 'How can we balance the core values of preserving freedom while limiting the harmful effects of racism?' (2011: 3).

This kind of tension recurs in what follows; however, this book is not centrally concerned with questions of regulation, as the extent of current conflicts concerning the public legitimacy of racist speech transcends, in significant ways, the parameters of legal considerations. Free speech is never simply a subject of law or a question of legality, and while the question of 'the limits of freedom of speech' is critically important, treating it as the singular horizon of discussion prevents a full engagement with the importance of 'free speech' as a political discourse and cultural imaginary in many contemporary societies. Freedom of speech is constantly invoked in public not solely as a legal principle, but because it acts as a focal point for advancing antagonistic visions of who constitutes the public and what values should guide public discourse.

Consider, as a point of entry, this fake political quotation from a list published on the popular US satirical site, McSweeney's Internet Tendency:

'We shall crush apartheid and white racist minority rule in the marketplace of ideas', Nelson Mandela, 1980. (Appel 2019)

What's the joke, exactly? It is said that you ruin a joke by explaining it; however, satire sharp enough to introduce some of the key issues analysed in this book can probably withstand some extended discussion. Mandela's personal history is well known to be marked by the brutal repression meted out by the apartheid regime. Opposition to apartheid involved mass mobilization, civil disobedience and international solidarity action. Laid out in these terms, the joke seems to rest on nothing more than an absurd juxtaposition – the dismantling of white supremacist rule was not secured through a free exchange of ideas. The satire, however, goes further. The phrase 'marketplace of ideas' is a prevalent metaphor in public discourse for what is often termed the *instrumental* value of free speech. Instrumental arguments for free speech base its value on the good it potentially produces: more truth, greater understanding, advances in knowledge, informed citizenship and so forth. Any arbitrary restriction on speech, therefore, risks distorting the diversity of opinion and processes of exchange through which better and truer ideas may emerge. The market is both metaphor and model for optimum democratic exchange, for if speech is left unhindered, the truth emerges as a kind of product from competition between ideas.

In the next chapter, it will become clear why this kind of free speech imaginary is intensely disputed from a variety of theoretical and political positions. The question, for now, is why the satirical intent is trained on the question of racism. The parody hinges on the assumption that racism can be 'defeated' in the marketplace of ideas because of how racism is dominantly understood as a product of ideas, and ideology. Consequently, racist ideas, like all ideas, are regarded as being open to forms of rational, deliberative engagement in the public sphere, where they can be disproven or discredited. In *Race: A Philosophical Introduction*, Paul C. Taylor regards this emphasis on ideas and attitudes as fundamental to contemporary confusion and conflict as to how racism is understood and spoken about in public:

> Defining 'racism' is difficult in part because we use the word to describe many different things. Some of us speak of racist people, actions, attitudes, and beliefs; others speak of racist practices, ideologies, and institutions. Some of us refuse to complain of racism unless there is some intentional discrimination; others are willing to set aside intentions and focus on consequences. Some of us want to think of racism as a matter of prejudice in individual interactions; others insist that it is about social systems and structures of power. (2013: 31)

This stark divergence is informed by many factors, but one of them is a pronounced narrative about the historical status of 'race' and racism, and this is where the satire hardens considerably. Apartheid South Africa stands as the last of the 'overtly racist regimes' of the twentieth century (Fredrickson 2002), and when arrayed against the awesome power of an historically symbolic racist state, faith in the power of reasoned persuasion appears absurd. However, after the end of such organized supremacist, racialized hierarchies, the dominant assumption in western public cultures is that racism is defined by what *remains*: ideas and ideology, manifested in forms of recognizably extremist politics and aberrant individual attitudes. In this 'postracial' context, such faith is not absurd, but self-evident, as these ideas and attitudes can and should be debated, the better to expose them, and to demonstrate the kind of tolerance that, so the story goes, racists lack.

Except, this is not self-evident to people who are subject to racism, and who struggle to describe and contest it in terms adequate to their experience and political goals. Racism, in Ambalavaner Sivanandan's well-known formulation, 'does not stay still', but is articulated differently according to changes in the economy, social structure and political formation (1990). The divergent understandings in Taylor's summary picture, therefore, are not just differences of opinion or an assorted collection of 'ideas'. They are politically consequential assumptions given meaning through structures, institutions and practices. Nor are these positions equivalent in their influence. The conviction that racism is primarily about ideas, attitudes and ideologies can be regarded as a 'post-war hegemonic ideology' in western nation-states with official, publicly renewed commitments to particular forms of anti-racism (Wade 2015: 1292).

Read against this backdrop, the pitch of McSweeney's satire is utterly contemporary. Conflicts over how racism is defined and how it is best opposed, and who gets to decide this and why, have erupted with renewed intensity in recent years, and they are often mediated through the question of 'free speech'. The headlines proclaiming a 'free speech crisis' survey arenas and institutions such as universities, mainstream journalistic outlets, political platforms and social media spaces, and often propose that the problem is a 'new intolerance' – a 'fragile' refusal to engage in democratic debate, to give ideas a fair hearing, and to respect the earlier described instrumental value of free speech. Increasingly, it is contended that there is a willingness to define racism with such elasticity – attaching it to any number of events and actions – that it shuts down legitimate debate and limits the diversity of acceptable viewpoints; the definition of racism, according to the political commentator David

Goodhart, 'has been subject to mission creep' (2017). Anti-racism, it is argued, has become a censorious political reflex, or in the proposition of a debate hosted by *Reason* magazine, 'the message of antiracism has become as harmful a force in American life as racism' (Gillespie 2018). Short of a frequently invoked and rarely defined threshold of 'hate speech', a refusal to engage with the free flow of ideas is regarded as a refusal of democratic values and procedure.

It is precisely this willingness to regard racist discourse as open to persuasion and deliberation that the egregiously faked Mandela quote takes issue with. Across these sites and arenas, people subject to forms of racism and those in solidarity with them are refusing to validate and amplify racist ideas by engaging with them *as ideas*. What kind of pluralism demands, as a common contemporary anti-racist slogan puts it, 'that I debate my humanity'? What understanding of democratic deliberation insists that those racialized as not white, or as 'migrant', or as 'Muslim', must treat the established logics and tropes of racist discourse as propositions for reasoned engagement, as if the world starts afresh with every new debate? What vision of 'the public' requires those racialized as 'problem populations' to validate the terms and frameworks of debates about 'the problem'? Lost in the sensationalist framing of free speech as 'in crisis' is the tension that the McSweeney quote captures acutely: that how one understands racism inevitably has consequences for how one conceptualizes free speech, and vice versa.

Given the insistent frenzy of crisis headlines, the contours of crisis have begun to receive critical attention, notably the tendency of appropriating 'free speech' as a shield against criticism or as a licence to provoke. Examining the 'weaponization' of free speech in Australian politics, Katharine Gelber observes that 'never before has the catch cry of "free speech" been used by so many so often as a catalyst for wider political objectives, many of which have very little to do with free speech at all' (2017). Surveying, in a *Guardian* Long Read essay, a narrative of crisis in the UK, William Davies points out how the 'claim that free speech is under attack is often a mask for other political frustrations and fears', and the unrestrained donning of this mask by 'conservative provocateurs' means that 'the ideal of free speech is being stretched to the point where the phrase starts to mean too much' (2018). In everyday Internet culture, the elastic instrumentalization they chart is parodied as 'freeze peach' – a presumed entitlement to speak without criticism, restraint or consequence.

One interpretation of this rhetorical appropriation of free speech is that it provides a way of occupying space and attention in highly mediated public cultures. Claiming that one has been 'silenced' is patently about generating publicity within the accelerated dynamics of the attention economy, and consequently all sorts of 'contrarians' seek to trigger secondary debates about their right to speech, in the service of anti-egalitarian goals. These voluble claims of silencing are made, generically, across the range of issues condescendingly bundled into the idea of 'culture war'. Political correctness, militant feminism, 'diversity police', the 'gay lobby', 'trans ideology', the multicultural consensus: projecting these as hegemonic is a well-established move, opening political space by inflating any opposition into evidence of repressive orthodoxy (Ahmed 2009). It is a transparent yet regularly efficient means of parlaying established public status into virtuous marginality, casting discredited ideas as deliberative propositions, reframing familiar, reactionary ideas as iconoclastic experiments, and entangling criticism and opposition in abstracted debates about freedoms that are not, in reality, substantially in question.

These tactics enable the recuperation of racist ideas and claim space for racist discourse, and as is discussed subsequently, they are not just opportunistic, but increasingly patterned into a financed and organized infrastructure of 'open debate' that, for all the declarations of scholarly and citizenly disinterestedness, is thoroughly preoccupied with race. This opportunism, nonetheless, is not sufficient to explain the contemporary intersection between racism and free speech. What is most at stake here is the shape rather than limits of speech in intensively mediated, multicultural societies. Thus, sketching out a corrective, normative theory of free speech will not tell us much about why racism is so often at the heart of these conflicts.

It is the central argument of this book that where racism is dominantly understood in terms of ideology and ideas, invocations of free speech have become fundamental to reshaping how racism is expressed and legitimized in public culture. As subsequent chapters demonstrate, this politics has many overlapping strands. Cumulatively, they fuel recurrent public controversies and media spectacles, where the right to express racist ideas and circulate racist discourse is increasingly marked out as what is most at stake in relation to freedom of speech. Yet what is principally at play in these disputes is not a legal right to speak or freedom from coercion. Instead, it is the legitimacy of what is being said, and the contested reception it receives in diverse, antagonistic and reactive public spheres. In contexts where there is intense political contestation and public confusion as to what constitutes racism, and who gets to define it, *free speech* has been adopted as a primary mechanism for validating, amplifying and reanimating racist ideas and racializing claims.

Free speech: the map and the territory

Freedom of speech is a central modern imaginary. In public discourse it is celebrated as a fundamental liberty; however, a dominant version of this celebration mistakes sacralization for political commitment, marginalizing the complexity of how 'speech' is organized and distributed. In some ways, this tension is not new. In the – capacious – liberal tradition with which freedom of speech is profoundly associated, it is primarily predicated on negative liberty, that is, freedom from arbitrary restriction or interference, particularly that of state and governmental power. In other, materialist and critical traditions, this dominant liberal vision has always been shadowed by the constraints it neglects: the forms of material possibility, structured inequality, political power, media access and communicative capacity that organize the meaningful distribution of expression and attention in racially ordered capitalist societies.

What is new, arguably, is a widespread cultural attachment to critically vacuous abstractions about free speech. This has become more pronounced even as the communicative landscape becomes more complex, and the forms of politics it amplifies become more marked in social and political life. In contemporary media debates, freedom of speech is regularly invoked in absolutist terms, shorn of its complex intersections with competing rights and interests. In political rhetoric, it is often claimed, reductively, as a defining feature of cultural and civilizational identities. In the churn of social media exchange, it is too often celebrated with dogged simplicity, with fake Voltaire quotes about 'defending to the death your right to say it' providing a sheltering meme for all Twitter storms. In this context, critically questioning how freedom of speech is understood is easily dismissed as being 'anti-free speech', or as demonstrating insufficient fidelity to what is assumed to be a settled principle. Yet, as the philosopher Alan Haworth has pointed out, the dogmatic fragments that decorate free speech debates '… began life in the context of an argument. Treating them as mere slogans will only set you on the wrong road' (1998: 50). For Haworth, 'invocations of abstract philosophical principle' (ibid.) avoid the difficult work of securing the grounds for freedom of speech by examining how well 'old maps' continue to 'match the lie of the land'.

Similarly drawing on spatial metaphors, Anshuman A. Mondal (2018) argues that 'modern liberal free speech theory' conceives of liberty as extending across a single homogenous plane. This landscape is flat and smooth, and, ideally, as you move across it, you should not encounter any obstacles until you hit its outer limits, which are the 'legitimate restraints on liberty' enacted by law and institutions. Any bump and disruption that you do encounter constitutes an infringement, or censorship. The problem with this unidimensional idea of freedom is that it drastically simplifies the map of a complex topography marked by features that shape, obstruct and enable communication. Freedom of expression does not simply extend cross a smooth plane until it meets given limits, but flows, like liquid, through an 'irregular and uneven terrain', and thus the freedom of discourse is 'not one of being or not being free, of having or not having free speech' (2018: 509).

Topographical features on this terrain, Mondal notes, correspond to the relative density and malleability of geographical features, where the heavy mass of law, institutions and the state forces detours while being changed slowly, often imperceptibly, whereas norms, values, culture and ideology are moulded by the flows they shape. Many such topographical features – media

forms, journalistic conventions, institutional procedures, social media platform affordances – feature in
the analysis to follow. And, as chapter 3's discussion of
the post-9/11 'Good Muslim/Bad Muslim' dichotomy
illustrates, Mondal's metaphorical approach is useful
for understanding how racializing practices can work
to effectively mute and throttle political speech – in
this instance, by young Muslim activists – in perfectly
legal ways. In working towards this, it is necessary to
start examining why flows of racial discourse achieve
such a strange viscosity on this terrain. This requires
thinking further on the polarized understandings of
racism outlined by Paul C. Taylor, and compressed in
the knowing exaggeration of McSweeney's historical
licence.

Racism as a public keyword

Scholarship on racism is characterized by a tension
between the theoretical complexity the idea generates
and the stark realities of subjugation and humiliation
it conjures up. This tension is inevitable, as racism is
not a universal theory. Historical and situated, it is
given shape through shifting political practices, social
relations and ideological inputs. The historicity of

racism extends to the term itself, as it is a relatively recent term for the hierarchical and differentialist work of *race* in structuring social relations in colonial modernity, and naturalized belonging in the ethnicized 'community' of the European nation-state (Hesse 2004). This historical, variable character pushes us to examine racism's articulation in and through capitalist relations, particular political ideologies, social antagonisms, national imaginaries and forms of representation (Virdee 2014). This analysis can be neither general nor discrete, but must be 'relational', paying attention to how particular populations are racialized in specific historical conjunctures, through practices and ideas that circulate across national borders (Goldberg 2015).

The complexity of how racism is understood in public culture is of a somewhat different order. Racism, as an *ism*, invites categorical sifting, into racism and not racism, racist and not racist (as if these categories alone can contain and organize the complexity of racial meaning). It seems to suggest a general theory, or at least require unitary meaning. The suggestive suffix notwithstanding, this unstable fixity is, to an important degree, a product of recent history. It is a consequence of a particular chronological narrative dominant in western nation-states that publicly declare and renew their commitments to anti-racism. Following the defeat of fascism, and in the aftermath of the Holocaust, both popular rejection of fascist politics, and state and institutional efforts to repudiate the idea of race, resulted in the marginalization of politics explicitly committed to hierarchical, scientifically inflected ideas of racism (Camus and Lebourg 2017). The discrediting of this idea of race, and of regimes, movements and past contexts that have come to symbolize the totality of racism, has contributed to a prevalent sense that racism is, if not thoroughly of the past, then defined by its pasts.

The narrowing of what is recognized as racism, or what can be articulated through the idea of racism, is politically consequential. Barnor Hesse unfurls these consequences, arguing that 'Since the ending of the US civil rights movement, the Cold War and the apartheid regime in South Africa, political discussion of the meaning of racism seems to be over in the West. Its sociality is overwhelmingly conceived as a problem that has largely been overcome' (2004: 10). The dominant post-war association of racism with *remnants*, extremist movements, or – frequently class-inflected – anachronistic forms of individual ignorance make it 'inconceivable or inadmissible', as Hesse continues, 'that racism could be a more enduring presence than its banishment to obsolescence would have us believe'

(2004: 10). This narrative summary indexes a hugely involved history, or better, set of related histories. Its value, nonetheless, is that it emphasizes how the historically important rejection of race as a set of pseudo-biological ideas, or a 'social construct' about the genetic basis for human differences, has produced contradictory effects in relation to the enduring force of race as practice and as 'social fact' (Roediger 2008). Race was never articulated through any one dominant ideological route, and the genocidal prominence of scientifically derived racial hierarchies did not preclude other forms of cultural, social and religious legitimation informing the sifting and ordering of populations in relation to a white European norm.

What is at stake, therefore, in the polarized usages outlined by Taylor can now be underlined more fully. Constricted, dehistoricized understandings of racism have made it possible to extract racism from political economy and social structures, locating it principally in the realm of ideas, such as movement ideologies and individual prejudices, which then manifest in the world as racist acts. The work of racialized logics in capitalist exploitation, through structural continuities in society and institutional procedures of the state, and through the shifting state-political modes of racialization that produce 'problem populations' in need of some form of management or intervention, is difficult to name as racism in this narrowing of permissible meanings.

Anti-racist movements and actions, of course, have never been dependent on agreed definitions of racism in public culture. Any definition of racism is necessarily political and a site of political contest, and anti-racism has been enacted and articulated in ways that do not depend on centring, discursively, practically or symbolically, the idea of racism. Nevertheless, anti-racism also requires identifying affinities and similarities in the experiences and histories of racialization inflicted on different populations through dispossession, exploitation, securitization, exclusion and conditional, coercive inclusion. As a public politics, this is forced to reckon with how, as Alana Lentin (2016) has argued, the dominant, 'frozen' sense of racism organizes the adjudication of contemporary racisms against 'past events that have been sanctioned for identification as racist'.

The status of frozen racism as *something that nearly everyone agrees is bad* hides the enduring continuities and variations in racist structures and practices after 'the conceptual erasure of race' (Goldberg 2015: 152). Hence the centrality of the question of denial to contemporary theories of race and racism: the categorical assumption that, shy of explicit forms of racist discourse or 'hate speech' that transgress social norms, what is in question must be something other than racism. This repeat dynamic is both an everyday and a spectacular occurrence. When Donald Trump proclaimed that the Democratic Party Representatives Ilhan Omar and Alexandria Ocasio-Cortez should 'go back and help fix the … crime-infested places from which they came', political debate and press coverage cycled around whether his remarks were 'racist'. Commentators such as Gary Abernathy in *The Washington Post* argued that this accusation was a tragedy, because *it brought race into it*, demonstrating how racism was a 'previously significant term being made frivolous by its abuse' (2019).

As the next chapter discusses, these dynamics go a long way to explaining the difficulties of speaking about racism. To understand the integration of free speech into these processes, it is important to underline the extent to which denial and dissolution are politically productive, operating across scales of activity, while also intensively contested in contemporary public cultures. The networked media ecology has vastly increased the range and scope of racist actors and the circulation of racist discourse, discourse that has, for decades, been honed to promote racialized meaning while deflecting the 'accusation' of racism (see chapter 4). Yet this ecology has also accelerated the pluralization of public cultures and extended the capacities of anti-racist counter-publics to respond, critique and organize. Within this diversified if not democratized media environment, 'discursive power' is in flux, distributed across platforms and subject to shifting practices of control and release (Jungherr et al. 2019). This discursive flux ensures that the meaning and salience of racism are a focus of constant conflict, strung between the expressive denial of racism, and the political desire of people who are subject to racism to describe and contest it in terms adequate to their experience and political struggle.

In the argument of this book, this incessant debating and defining are regarded as a generative dimension of the politics of racism in irreducibly diverse societies dominantly imagined as both 'white' and anti-racist. And it is under these conditions of flux and paradox, of capacious denial and renewed contestation, of incessant discourse as to what constitutes racism and who gets to decide, that 'free speech' has been drawn into validating, amplifying and reanimating racist ideas and racializing claims.

Closure, culture, capture

In this book I propose three dimensions of this politics for analysis, treated sequentially over the three chapters that follow. These dimensions are, inevitably, deeply interconnected. The thematic shape they are given here focuses on how racism is animated through free speech politics, and what is consequently at stake for under-standings of freedom of speech.

The first dimension examines what could be described as the paradox of *closure* in relation to racialized knowledge in putatively postracial societies. That is, in societies where racism is broadly regarded as 'a thing of the past', racialized knowledge, artefacts and discourses continually resurface, as potentially innocent, as test cases of public toleration, across sites and genres of expression. The ironic humour of hipster racism, the scholarly case for colonialism, the merits of racial science, the childish fun of blackface: rituals of public debate form around these often intensively mediatized controversies, and pivot on adjudicating whether 'this is racism or not'. Consequently, the experience of racism is reduced to just another opinion in this adjudication, and the historical accumulation of racialized discourse to just another stream in the free flow of ideas. Understanding these dynamics is key to grasping how anti-racism's insistence on certain forms of closure is increasingly presented as a threat to free speech, that is, as an arbitrary restriction on disinterested enquiry and exchange in the public sphere.

The second surveys the racializing work performed by freedom of speech when it is designated as an essential property or exclusive achievement of *culture.* This has become particularly pronounced in the cultural politics of security and 'integration' dominant in the post-9/11 context. Over the last two decades, anti-Muslim racism – across a range of political tendencies – frames 'the Muslim' as a figure of implacable cultural difference, gendered threat and value-based incompatibility. Respect for freedom of speech has emerged as a primary marker of *integratability.* In a corollary of the logic of the 'war on terror', it is increasingly presented in absolutist terms: you are either for freedom of speech, or you are not. The respect demanded, however, is not that of demonstrating respect for political freedom, but that of displaying the correct attitude towards 'our' democracy. At the same time, this cultural demand for respect for freedom of speech obscures the ways in which political speech that challenges powerful regimes or institutions has been drastically limited in this same period. This raises the question as to how and why, under these political conditions, certain issues come to be persuasively framed as freedom of speech issues, and others do not.

The third considers the *capture* of free speech by the political far right as a mechanism for recuperating and amplifying racist discourse. Denial is not just produced through hegemonic assumptions about the absence of racism, or effected by restricting the public space in which racist structures and practices can be questioned. It is also an expressive structure, the scaffolding through which ideological articulations of racism have been refashioned over the last decades. The horizon of 'frozen racism' has for decades ensured that, as Sivamohan Valluvan puts it, 'racist discourses always masquerade as being claims of a different order' (2016: 2246). The discussion of capture, consequently, deals with how ideological claims are currently articulated. Far-right movements in Europe and the US have long established histories of appropriating the language of civil liberties and human rights to legitimate the form, if not the content, of their actions. The capture of free speech aims to create space for racist speech as a beleaguered expression of liberty, but it goes further.

It makes instrumental claims for the value of that speech as a 'taboo' truth, a truth rendered unfree by the official hegemony of anti-racism. In the current political moment, where neo-fascist parties and movements seek to animate 'reactionary nationalist, racist, gendered and religious identities' (Camp et al. 2019), the claim that their freedom of speech is denied through the repression of truth is more than merely hypocrisy, or opportunism. The hallmark of the putative 'post-truth' era is not just the proliferation of competing 'truths', but the structuring force of the reactionary contention that there is a truth, and it is being repressed. The capture of 'free speech' by a diverse range of ideological projects on the political far right requires examining the cultural and political work that the invocation of free speech performs when tied to the disputed legitimacy of racist ideas in public culture, and when implicated in the regeneration of racist logics.

TWO

Closure: who decides what is racist?

Introduction

In societies convinced of their postracial status, racism is always something else, and happens somewhere else. In news headlines it is a suspended sentence, held in the noncommittal quarantine of inverted commas. In political life it is an accusation, refuted through tears, character references and the timely production of the best of friends. In public discussion it is a subject of competitive definition, as interlocuters adjudicate whether or to what extent an utterance corresponds to easily googled delineations of what is, and what definitively is not, racism. Increasingly, in public discourse, it is cast as an arbitrary full stop, a 'silencing word' that shuts down debate, restricts a diversity of opinion, and embargoes what are inevitably presented as uncomfortable truths. In the gap between the widespread rejection of 'frozen racism', and the efforts of those who experience racism to give an account of its contemporary manifestations, the meaning of racism has become a site of intensely public conflict.

In *Are we all postracial yet?*, David Theo Goldberg notes this as a paradox of the 'postracial moment', where 'race is supposed to be a thing of the past. And yet all we do, seemingly, is to talk about it' (2015: 1). In his argument, this incessant talk is symptomatic of postraciality's confusions, of how 'racist expression can thrive at the very moment that racial configuration is claimed to be a thing of the past' (2015: viii). Though replete with confusion, postracialism is an active socio-political process, where what is at work is 'the restructuring of the conditions of racist expression, and their terms of articulation' (2015: 113). The focus of this chapter is on this 'postracial talk', its dynamics of denial and contestation, and why these 'debates' as to the meaning and salience of racism so often produce free speech controversies. While these debates spin off in multiple directions, it is possible to suggest a structuring antagonism. Understandings of racism in public discourse are political; forged through political action, they are mobilized, and argued and agitated for. At the same time, a key element of postracial presumption is substantive control of what racism means. Any contention beyond the ahistorical, moralized and pathologized 'normal definition' risks being deemed excessive because it calls into question what Fatima El-Tayeb, in *European Others*, examines as a galvanized sense of European and western exceptionalism:

> To reference race as native to contemporary European thought, however, violates the powerful narrative of Europe as a colorblind continent, largely untouched by the devastating ideology it exported all over the world. This narrative, framing the continent as a space 'free' of race (and, by implication, racism), is not only central to the way Europeans perceive themselves, but has also gained near-global acceptance. (2011: xv)

In variations on this narrative, some nations are 'freed' of racism. In Germany, the idea of racism is shaped by the profound association of race with the Nazi genocide, and consequently 'by the myth that Germans have successfully purged race thinking and racism from their society and politics after 1945' (Meng 2015: 123). In the United States, the 'narrative of triumph over racism as a defining feature of its society', Keeanga-Yamahtta Taylor argues, has gone through several iterations since the Civil Rights struggles of the 1950s and 1960s, with the hopeful mainstream assumption that the presidency of Barack Obama marked the definitive arrival of the 'postracial society' constituting the latest of these

transcendent achievements (2015). In France, propo-
nents of the universalism of the secular Republican state
situate the remainders of racism in perceived cultural
and ethnic particularism, be it the ethno-nationalism
of the capacious French right, or, in a telling equivalence, 'divisive' communal expression by racialized
minorities (Nadi 2017). Other nations, alternatively,
have always been 'free' of it: Gloria Wekker diagnoses
'white innocence' in the Netherlands as produced
through a splitting between the – imported, German
– antisemitism of the Holocaust and the disavowed
racism of Dutch colonialism, 'while a dominant
discourse stubbornly maintains that the Netherlands is
and always has been color-blind and antiracist, a place
of extraordinary hospitality and tolerance towards the
racialized/ethnicized other' (2016: 1).

Such thumbnail sketches tell little, of course, of
the ongoing reproduction of these imaginaries, or of
important counter-currents and disruptions. They do
indicate, nonetheless, that a presumption of national
innocence or exceptionalism provides a resilient
horizon for public discourse. Think, for example, of
how many public cultures are marked by often intensively mediated incidents and controversies – 'careless'
political remarks, witness videos to racist verbal and
physical attacks, 'misunderstood' jokes, contested

traditions – which ensure that the meaning of racism is a focus of constant debate and conflict. Almost inevitably, these incidents generate a storm of discourse as to what constitutes racism, and who gets to define it – storms which are often framed in the confidently unifying terms of an 'open debate' or 'national conversation about race'.

This chapter argues that we cannot understand how freedom of speech has become bound up in these 'conversations' without considering such postracial dynamics. Specifically, it examines a conflict centred on *closure*. With racism dominantly defined in terms of its pastness and exceptionalism, attempts to account for its shifting contemporary articulations are easily cast as 'defining everything as racism', and thus as shutting down public debate. An entry point to this conflict over closure is to examine some of the expectations invested in the ideal of public debate.

Let's just have the debate

The period following the 'Brexit' referendum in the UK was marked by many antagonisms in public discourse, including, in the context of an intensification in the politics of migration, bordering and legitimate belonging to the 'nation', a meta-debate on the salience of racism. In 2018, the comedian Tom Walker, better known for his satirical journalist character Jonathan Pie, appeared on Channel 4's *Ways to Change the World* programme, as one of several such high-profile appearances in this period where he argued that the 'rush to call out racism' posed a threat to free speech. An excerpt of Walker discussing freedom of speech with the presenter, Krishnan Guru-Murthy, was widely circulated by the broadcaster on social media:

> Freedom of speech is an immovable right for horrible people as well as nice people. If you're a horrible person, if you're a racist for example, I want to hear it. As long as you're not inciting hatred, as long as you're not inciting violence. If your opinion is that the colour of your skin makes you superior to me because of the colour of my skin you should be able to say it because then I can argue against you. If it's illegal for you to say it, it just bubbles up. So that's just the general level of what surely freedom of speech should be. (Walker 2018)

Walker's pithy comments are remarkable in their fidelity not only to the 'frozen' definition of racism but also to the vision of free speech criticized by Mondal, as ideally extending across the 'smooth surface' of liberty.

In the capacious liberal tradition, broadly two forms of argument are used to ground claims about the value of free speech. Moral arguments situate themselves within the intrinsic value of free speech to human autonomy. Consequentialist or instrumental arguments, as noted in the last chapter, predicate the value of unfettered speech on the democratic benefits that accrue from its free flow. In practice, as Walker demonstrates, both rationales interact: 'racists' have the right to express their racism within the boundaries dictated by laws on incitement to hatred, but they should also express their racism so that it can be debated and, as befits such false beliefs and irrational propositions, disproved.

Liberalism, as Michael Freeden has shown, is historically fluid and marked by a significant range of internal divergences and disagreements.[1] This vital plurality is often quieted, however, by contemporary liberalism's claim to be 'merely an expression of the ground rules of universal ethical conduct' (2008: 12). Arguably this claim is most pronounced in arguments such as Walker's for the 'general level' of what freedom of speech 'should be', assuming, as it does, that the only admissible public values are liberal ones. In this it draws on a powerful edifice of ideas about the relationship of democracy, debate and public reason. As Sophia Rosenfeld summarizes,

From John Milton well before the Age of Revolution
to John Stuart Mill well afterward, consequentialists
long justified a largely unrestricted realm of expression
… as a spur to the pursuit of truth. The idea was that
competition – among ideas, thinkers, texts – would, in
a world in which it was hard to be certain, ultimately
work to dispel errors in fact and interpretation alike
and to advance real knowledge, especially when it came
to religious or philosophical claims. (2019: loc. 436)

Faith in the 'epistemic and moral value of unfettered
debate' was critical not only to progress in the realms
of science and philosophy, but, as modern nation-states
took shape, to the production of public knowledge,
an informed citizenry, and thus the legitimacy of
representative democracy. Though mediated by the
institutions, laws and procedures of democratic states,
the freedom of citizens to receive and also debate
information and opinions would ensure a pluralism of
opinion and perspectives, and the formation of sound
judgements. This pluralism accords a special value to
minority opinions and heterodox ideas, not only as
intrinsic moral goods, but also as critical to the constant
reinvigoration of received ideas and settled dogma.[2] It is
this legacy that Walker draws on in fluently compressed
fashion – within the given realm of expression, all

ideas should be heard, no idea should be summarily excluded, and every idea can be debated.

It is not unfair to this body of thought to immediately point out, as Rosenfeld does, that it 'was never more than a rough ideal or set of ambitions' in the face of structural obstacles and power relations (2019: loc. 489). The idealized public of the bourgeois public sphere – the space of debate about matters of common concern – has long been critiqued for its abstraction from power relations (Fenton 2016). The idea of public deliberation as convened through the power of dialogue and persuasion has only withstood contact with a jagged topography of exclusion and obstruction, struggle and mobilization, by turning inwards and burnishing ideal-type processes of how publics *ought* to be.

Communication in the liberal public sphere is conceived of as transmission, conveying information and composed of reasoned arguments that can make persuasive claims on the basis of shared rationality. This privileging of rationality, its dependence on an individualistic, white, masculinized imaginary of the subject, and its universalistic conception of historical progress and public interest, has been a steady focus of poststructuralist, feminist and postcolonial critique (Braidotti 2013: 13–25). Advocates of 'robust debate', Davina Cooper observes, 'tend to treat speech as akin to a missile system, where discrete units of meaning pass back and forth between fully intentional, fixed subjects (whose interests, concerns and agenda are clear and prior to any engagement)' (2013). It has also been subject to more immanent lines of criticism. As Alan Haworth notes in his detailed reading of John Stuart Mill's *On Liberty*, Mill's prioritization of 'the liberty of thought and discussion' must assume, as a condition of possibility, the 'liberty of the seminar room'. That is, the consequentialist commitment to striving for truth through free expression, through advancing propositions and deliberating on them, examining competing views without arbitrary closure, requires the 'artificiality' of a seminar discussion, where there is 'tacit or explicit agreement amongst its members to a fairly complex set of conventions, rules and procedures' (1998: 28–9).

In general, there seems to be little difficulty accepting that the conditions of the seminar room do not hold in contemporary public cultures. 'Public communication', as Ari Adut argues, 'rarely takes the form of a debate with widespread, egalitarian dialogue' (2018: 10). This is not just because forms of 'bullshit' are a pronounced characteristic of intensively mediated public spheres, where opinion as commodity is as important for its 'exchange value' in capacious and accelerated media networks of comment and reaction as for its 'use value' in public deliberation (Dean 2009). It is also because intellectual engagement, shared reflection and meaningful discussion take place through modes of communication that may be more collaborative, or more antagonistic, than the institution of debate and its faith in the best ideas emerging from an adversarial exchange of arguments. Further, anyone that has experienced the feeling of togetherness that can emerge from collaborative group discussions, or the emotions stirred by fast-moving Twitter streams, is aware that communication engages us affectively and relationally in ways unaccounted for when speech is understood in primarily intellectual terms.

Depending on one's political and theoretical starting points, it is possible to locate some form of democratic potential in some or all of these communicative processes and modes of engagement. And scepticism towards reductively rationalistic ideas of deliberation and agency does not require 'denying that rationality can, and often does, constitute a crucial source of social emancipation' (Susen 2011: 54). Rather, the question for this chapter is why, on such a complex and contradictory communicative terrain, in which people regularly switch between discursive practices, values and contexts, the expectations of the seminar room are brought so assiduously and disproportionately to bear on debates about racism.

When racism is predominantly understood as irrational, and as an individual failing, its public treatment is inevitably categorical, hingeing on whether an act or utterance can be classified as racist, or not. Categorical, and moralistic: given a pronounced tendency in liberal argument to treat speech as an unmediated expression of thought and conscience (Gelber and Brison 2019), the burden of proof – beyond legal infringement or dicing with overt, 'classical' racism – falls on those levelling the *accusation*.[3] In the postracial rationale, to admit to or to be found holding such racist beliefs is 'effectively a declaration of one's moral degeneracy' (Pitcher 2009: 13). Yet it also means accepting, as Barnor Hesse notes in the situating narrative discussed in the last chapter, that 'political discussion of the meaning of racism seems to be over in the West' (2004: 10). For those that accept that this discussion is at an end, anti-racist attempts to capture how racism changes historically, to describe and oppose its shifting political expressions, appear ideologically suspect, presenting a moral hazard for open enquiry, free discussion and a presumption of argumentative good faith. This leads, as Alana Lentin argues, to significant investment in a stance of 'not racism', that is, that 'calling something racist' is only legitimate if it is based on 'the predominance of individualist moralism; the reliance on an overly narrow, strictly biological and hierarchical account of racism; and the universalisation of racism as equally practiced by all groups independent of status and power' (2018: 411). Anti-racist perspectives that are not confined to these elements restrict public discussion *because they refuse closure on what racism really means.*

In consequentialist understandings of freedom of speech, the idea of closure plays an important role. In representative democracies the 'marketplace of ideas' must provide the resources to make decisions, while also accepting that closure is necessary for decisions to be made. Closure in this understanding is tied to democratic procedures; when wider public issues are at stake, closure is undesirable as it encourages premature consensus, may be arbitrarily imposed, and stifles minority opinions and unorthodox ideas (for discussion see Ferree et al. 2002). This pronounced suspicion towards closure renders the contemporary liberal refusal to consider the historical and contextual shape of racism puzzling: why the insistence on the frozen in a model dedicated to free flow?

Perhaps the most familiar reason, given its centrality to public rituals about whether an utterance is racism or 'not racism', is the primacy placed on intent in the categorical-moral definition. Commenting on the media storm following Trump's tweets about the so-called 'squad' of Ilhan Omar, Alexandria Ocasio-Cortez, Ayanna Pressley and Rashida Tlaib (see chapter 1, p. 20). Ian G. Haworth argued that descriptions of his comments as racist lacked evidence of intent, and therefore the goal of such a slur is to 'invalidate the arguments of their opponents by labelling them as bigots, conveniently bypassing the need for substantive evidence, objective debate, or logical arguments' (2019). At first glance, the idea that Trump's suggestion – that the senators cannot be real Americans despite their birthplace and citizenship because of their 'immigrant backgrounds', a suggestion that only makes sense through an overt association between whiteness and Americanness – requires further 'objective debate' seems absurd. However, the same impulse is at work in Walker's determination to treat 'your hatred of the colour of my skin' as an (ir)rational proposition to be refuted, rather than as any other kind of speech act, or as speech that may have effects beyond an 'orientation to the truth'.

As this suggests, the categorical-moral definition depends on presenting a form of positivism as the only admissible yardstick for public claims-making. That is, if racism is fully located in ideas and ideology, and expressed through intentional speech acts and actions, it can and should be proven to be racism or 'not racism'. This has become a central concern of some public commentators in the UK, concerned, like Walker, that an imprecise and expansive notion of racism has distorted public debate on immigration in the UK, rendering 'taboo' all expressions of national feeling or group partiality, particularly in the context of national divisions over 'Brexit'. It may be, as Eric Kaufmann states in pursuing his thesis that 'white racial self-interest is not racism', that racism exists in 'new hidden guises'; however, 'the problem is that such arguments are unfalsifiable' (2017: 11). To deal with the problem of 'expansive definition', he draws a hard distinction between rational 'ethno-demographic interests' and 'an irrational fear or hatred of the other'.

This 'over-reach of the concept', David Goodhart argues, requires an 'agreed definition of the word', and he proceeds to define 'proper' racism as 'an irrational hostility based on race, usually accompanied by a belief in the superiority or inferiority of certain races'. Given that racism in this description, he continues, is 'either literally illegal or at least illegitimate in British society', racist acts can be verified against legal transgressions and widespread moral sanction (2014: 251–3). In the widely publicized assessment of these writers, any attempt to exceed these definitional boundaries is at best unscientific, and at worst a foreclosing of debate that chills free speech through fear of the wrong kind of moral sanction. On these grounds, closure on the definition of racism is necessary to promote the general openness of free expression.

An extended example from this same period in Britain helps in thinking through the implications of this insistence on the closure of definition. Four days after Walker's interview was broadcast, the UK Home Secretary Amber Rudd resigned as a consequence of the 'Windrush scandal', so called because people who moved from the Commonwealth Caribbean to Britain between 1948 and 1971 had, since 2014, been increasingly detained, denied access to social rights, made unemployed and even deported because they could not prove their right to live in Britain. The British Nationality Act of 1948 had allowed colonial subjects to move as British citizens; however, the target-driven 'hostile environment policy' of 2014 onwards, designed to make residence in Britain as difficult as possible for anyone with an 'irregular migration' status, ensnared this generation and their children in a system of immigration status checks and deeply punitive procedures because they could not produce cursory paperwork issued half a century before. 'Windrush migrants' and 'illegal migrants' have a 'shared vulnerability to state violence and racism', Luke de Noronha argues, because 'the law changes around people; *illegality is produced* in ways which create divisions within our families, communities and classrooms' (2018, italics in original). As he notes, these events help demonstrate how 'the immigration regime shapes and produces racial meanings and racist practices in the present' (2019: 2).

According to the threshold set by the tenets of 'not racism', de Noronha's contention is puzzling. Political reaction to the scandal was at pains to underline the legitimate belonging of those affected: 'they are British, they are part of us', as the then Prime Minister Theresa May told the House of Commons. Further, the claim of a 'shared vulnerability' to racism is belied by the political response, which distinguished between Black British victims 'caught up in our review' and those subject to detention and deportation as a consequence of their illegal status, not their 'race'. For the custodians of definition, therefore, casting the net of racism too wide risks, once again, foreclosing public debate through indiscriminate usage.

The problem with this position, however, is that de Noronha's analysis is predicated not on adjudicating the categorical content of a political statement or act, but on thinking systemically, understanding racism as articulated historically with and through other relations, structures and antagonisms that cannot be encompassed by a singular, universalist definition, and where its effects matter independently of whether 'motives' can be established, or not. In *Traces of History: Elementary Structures of Race* (2016), Patrick Wolfe stresses the need to avoid assuming the 'uniform workings of a discursive monolith called race' in colonial modernity, and instead to examine its 'thematic content' in relation to race as active production:

> Ideology is, therefore, only part of the story, albeit an important one. In addition to noting race's development as an organised narrative or doctrine, we need to observe it in operation, as a set of classificatory regimes that seek to order subject populations differentially in pursuit of particular historical agendas. To this extent the term 'racism' seems redundant, since race already is an 'ism'. As performed and contested on the ground ... race emerges not as singular or unified but as a fertile, Hydra-headed assortment of local practices. To express this applied versatility, we may distinguish between race as doctrine ... and racialisation as an assortment of local attempts to impose classificatory grids on a variety of colonised populations to particular though coordinated ends. (2016: 10)

It is this attention to how race in action is not limited to or represented by racist ideology that de Noronha brings to bear on the active production of illegality, and thus the ordering of populations, by the state. The shifting spectrum of contingent immigration statuses actively exposes people to the coercive power of the state; to classifications which activate forms of surveillance, exclusion from services, separation from society, and ultimately deportation from the national territory. These practices of 'bordering' may be bolstered by public discourse and discriminatory acts; however, the active production of race through immigration apparatuses is not driven by discourse or substantiated by 'uncovering racially discriminatory immigration enforcement practices'. Racialized distinctions are produced by immigration procedures and practices, not settled prior to them. For example, de Noronha demonstrates how under Operation Nexus, UK police officers cooperate with immigration officials to secure deportations for non-citizens who have not been convicted of crimes by supplying 'intelligence' on alleged criminality, particularly 'gang involvement', a move which integrates the policing of gangs into the 'deportation regime', thus increasing police surveillance of young black men 'despite young white men committing the vast majority of serious youth violence'

(2019: 14). While there are obvious continuities here with histories of discriminatory policing against black British men, this is not a static relation, as criminality, illegality and blackness, in this framework, dynamically reproduce each other. Race, in this understanding, is a technique of power, and 'always in formation'.

This shifting set of racializing practices cannot be adequately understood if analysis has to be accommodated to a 'definition of racism'. The kind of approach de Noronha exemplifies is not striving for a general theory, or seeking evidence of racism as a definitive motive. Those troubled by overly expansive 'definitions' of racism imagine them being dispatched to colonize public discourse, conquering outwards from a stable point of reference. The attention to relations and contingencies of race in formation indicates, to the contrary, that there is no flag to plant, as 'part of the complexity of analysing the historical impact of racism is that it is often intertwined with other social phenomena, and indeed can only be fully understood if we are to see how it works in specific social settings' (Murji and Solomos 2015: 10). To reduce racism to ideology and ideas, and to present ideology as discursively discrete and coherent, and something that individuals can be in transparent possession of, enacts a vicious circularity. The agreed definition is used to recognize that, and only that, which already corresponds to the terms and conditions of the definition.

This is where those who seek to police political discourse through proper, verifiable definitions get trapped, ironically, in the self-referentiality of discourse. The test of Goodhart's proper definition, remember, is whether or not an alleged racist statement or act can be verified as such against that which is 'already deemed illegitimate in British society'; for Kaufmann, it hinges on whether 'anti-immigration whites' consider their desire for lower immigration in order to protect their 'group position' to be racist or not. There is nowhere else to turn; this loop of verification is all that remains when the idea of racism as ideology is extracted from the historical forces and relations through which ideologies are produced. It depends on a 'bucket theory of mind' – to use Karl Popper's phrase – that, having ruled out social and political conditions and processes, has no way of explaining how individual buckets are replenished, beyond the glacial deposits of frozen ideas present in irrational thought and pathological behaviour. On such weak foundations, it seems hard to sustain the idea that 'freedom of thought and discussion' is being curtailed *tout court* by attempts, no matter how profoundly one might disagree with them, to describe how racism works, in public discussion normatively oriented to understanding how society functions and changes. It seems equally hard to insist on closure as to the meaning of racism when one's preferred definition is revealed as nothing more than a product of extensive, undeclared foreclosure.

Dynamics of the debatable

In her 2017 book *Why I'm No Longer Talking to White People about Race*, Reni Eddo-Lodge refuses to debate:

> I'm no longer engaging with white people on the topic of race. Not all white people, just the vast majority who refuse to accept the legitimacy of structural racism and its symptoms. ... They truly believe that the experiences of their life as a result of their skin colour can and should be universalised. Amid every conversation about Nice White People feeling silenced by conversations about race, there is a sort of ironic and glaring lack of understanding or empathy for those of us who have been visibly marked out as different for our entire lives, and live the consequences. It's truly a lifetime of self-censorship that people of colour have to live. (2017: ix–xii)

Eddo-Lodge's point about universalization provides a sharp corrective to Walker's thought experiment, hingeing, as it does, on his self-positioning as liberalism's 'generic colorless political subject' (Mills 2017: 6) that dispassionately engages in an imagined debate, fully bracketed from the histories of racialization which have freighted skin colour with meaning. In the prevalent liberal gatekeeping of proper dialogue, to speak from experience in this way is regarded as essentialist and thus as another way of 'shutting down debate', but this is not Eddo-Lodge's position. In contrast to Walker's vision of the smooth surface, she etches further features into speech's mottled topography, noting the forms of foreclosure that trammel and shape the flow of discourse in lived practices and relations.

Liberal free speech formulations, in their reluctance to engage in questions of experience and subjectivity, language and structure, and power and materiality, can neglect how speech occurs in settings which shape what is said, and within interactive relations that inform the production of meaning. Speech is regulated by institutional provision (such as witnessing conventions in a courtroom), constrained through the disciplinary force of convention (the lecture form in a university), mediated by communicative infrastructures, gatekeepers and formats (who gets to speak as an expert, or 'ordinary person', in television debates), amplified or marginalized by political processes and dominant power relations (gendered assumptions about political leadership and who is 'worth listening to'), and calibrated in relation to the shifting boundaries of the permissible and the recognizable (presumed taboos, interpersonal discretion). The liberal emphasis on free speech as unhindered speech in the public domain elides how forms of closure are always at work across scales and domains of communication.

What Eddo-Lodge points to is how 'not racism' acts, in this topography, as a particular structure of contingent closure. Similarly, Sara Ahmed's work on institutional processes and social interactions explores what can occur in the gap between the 'official prohibition' of racism and the experience of racialized exclusions: 'It can be wilful to even name racism, as if the talk about divisions is what is divisive. Given that racism recedes from social consciousness, it appears as if the ones who "bring it up" are bringing it into existence ... It is as if talking about racism is what keeps it going' (2010). Ahmed and Eddo-Lodge write in an important tradition of examining how racism functions at different scales and intensities in lived experience. In so doing, they also underline the problem an expressive structure of denial poses for engaging in public discourse. What does it mean, and what does it demand, to enter into 'debate' where 'not racism' seeks to set the terms of reference and engagement? Silencing, as Eddo-Lodge and Ahmed describe it, operates through the reproduction of postracial suppositions which must be repeatedly navigated while never being openly declared, a practical structure of closure which raises questions as to the personal cost and political value of engaging in putatively open debates. Reflecting on the media dynamics of the Brexit period, the journalist Kuba Shand-Baptiste argued that the ceaseless exposure of women of colour to public formats where it is a requirement to 'justify our own existence' is increasingly resulting in 'the deliberate exodus from our broadcast media of exactly the voices we need to hear more of' (2020).

It is important to consider how these stakes are raised through the discursive churn of a networked media ecology predicated on the competition for attention. Competing understandings of racism are circulated in a communicative environment that systemically refuses closure, generating 'debate' as a structural driver of content dissemination and attention capture. In particular, these conflicted understandings are increasingly circulated and contested in the everyday cultures of connective media, through platforms which are dependent on the production of discourse as a commercial and structural imperative. Miri Song, in her work on how Twitter discussions on racism in the UK are driven by public controversies, has linked this prerogative of circulation to what she terms a 'culture of racial equivalence', where public understandings of racism are 'often highly imprecise, broad, and used to describe a wide range of racialized phenomena' (2014: 108). A consequence of this is a general sense of racism as prejudice, and thus the 'growing tendency in Britain to regard almost any form of racial statement, made by anyone (of any hue), as automatically, and indiscriminately, "racist"' (2014: 111). For Song, the consequences of this 'conceptual inflation' are serious, as the idea of racism is stripped of its 'historical basis, severity and power', and racialized experiences are relativized and silenced.

This imprecision or inflation is more than a consequence of the terms of postracial assumption being given expression on social media. It is also indicative of how racism's endless disputability is amplified by media dynamics and platform logics. The logics that Song describes are also produced within a media system driven by a commercial logic to generate comment, and to multiply options to interact, reply, pass judgement, spread opinions and *debate*. In these circuits of discourse, there can never be closure on a 'reasonable definition'. This is not just because of the irreducibly political contest as to what racism means, but also because structures of circulation eschew closure, rendering every question and issue continuously open to debate. Equivalence is produced because the very mention of racism is generative – every utterance is an invitation to discourse, every comment a potential proposition to refute, every statement a trigger for amplification.

This rationale has been given algorithmic expression in structures of 'content management'; several inves-tigations into Facebook moderation procedures have demonstrated how African Americans writing about the racism they have experienced on the platform have had their posts removed or accounts suspended for contravening 'community standards' (Sankin 2017). That is, discussing the experience of racism becomes the racism which is sanctioned. Its synthesis with routines of journalistic balance also feeds an amplificatory logic. When the hashtag #WhiteProverbs trended in the US, UK and Australia in 2014 it worked through a particular memetic form: that of an ironic 'white' voice innocently reproducing forms of racism denial – 'I don't see colour. White proverb.' Contrary to the assumption that the restricted nature of social media forms militates against expressive insight, the satirical recasting of the proverb form provided a way of illustrating the resilience of the 'not racism' suppositions that permeate debate. Yet hashtags circulate transnationally, inviting and inciting discourse at a velocity determined by whether Twitter 'throttles' or 'promotes' them. By the time the hashtag was picked up and framed by BBC News' 'Trending' feature, it had been hijacked by accusations of 'anti-white racism' and consequently reclaimed to the logic of equivalence as expressed in the BBC's proposition for online debate: 'But does a hashtag like this actually contribute to any real progress in race relations, or is it just a way to make white people feel bad about things they say, perhaps innocently?'

The rapidly shifting dynamics of this example are illustrative of the challenges involved in reconceptualizing ideas of public dialogue under conditions of communicative abundance. The view from the seminar room rarely accounts for the communicative conditions under which discussions take place. When it does, there is a tendency to turn the dial to dystopia, as exemplified in the narrative of the death of 'public dialogue', interred in a procession of 'echo chambers'. The techno-deterministic story of fracture by 'filter bubble' is too static and incurious, offering a seductive metaphor rather than an account of what people actually do with media in their everyday practices. The image of neatly siloed and atomized consumers evades the real challenge of analysing contemporary publics, which are, as Ingrid Volkmer argues, characterized by fluid and dynamic 'public densities' that form in and across social media platforms and discursive sites. These are, according to Volkmer, bursts of 'connected discursive consciousness' that emerge from communicative actors 'reproducing, delivering, accelerating and magnifying content within the chosen logics of subjective networks across a globalized scope' (2014: 3).

These densities, like #WhiteProverbs, may provide 'resonance spaces', that is, 'spaces of simultaneous reasoning across lively communicative domains' (2014: 10). They may also, again like #WhiteProverbs, variously or simultaneously be shaped by social media's circuits of drive and frenzies of crowd-sourced cruelty. The Internet and digital media are deeply ambivalent (Philips and Milner 2017). As Herman Gray argues, the increasingly complex media ecosystem is 'where social relations, representations, understandings and feelings about racial differences among us circulate' (Gray 2017: 163). The partial reordering of media gatekeeping and the reduction of significant barriers to entry have certainly engendered somewhat more pluralized public cultures, and the network dynamics of speed and circulation have extended the capacities of anti-racist counter-publics to respond, critique and organize. And, through the incessant, industrial production of speech – news, opinion, commentary, images, memes – space for the circulation and amplification of racist repertoires is vastly increased.

Precisely because the expectations of the seminar room have been so abrasively trained on 'the public conversation about racism', whether, when and how to engage with racializing discourse have emerged as a key antagonism in public culture, particularly and acutely for those *made into the subjects of debate*. Eddo-Lodge's book began as a widely shared blogpost, a reflection on what it means, in mediated interactions and interpersonal discussions, to be compelled to discuss racialized arrangements and relations on the terms set by 'not racism'. It is a refusal to accept postracial closure, centre exceptionalism, confirm equivalence, and give up on the struggle of those subjected to racism to define it politically. It is also a refusal of the logic of circulation whereby every passing talking point lays claim to the status of deliberative proposition. It recognizes the practical impossibility of discursive closure, and the ethical, tactical and political dilemmas that these conditions throw up incessantly.

It is not, evidently, a rejection of public communication. Its refusal is heuristic, oriented towards a broad public, inviting thinking about what kinds of engagement can transcend postracial enclosure, and whether a process of forming broadly shared under-standings of public speech and action can ever avoid erasing the lived realities of race. Viewed from the seminar room, to reject debate is to pre-emptively foreclose on the democratic necessity of a free flow of ideas. However, if postracialism is understood as 'the restructuring of the conditions of racist expression', this form of refusal is not a full stop, but a question mark. It is a pointed invitation to reflect on how boundaries to permissible speech are produced and policed, and a demand to forge minimal conditions of discursive viability under conditions of endless, ceaseless debate.

How this viability may be cultivated is a critical question because these communicative conditions are shaping an unsettling political reflex that secures further public space for racist discourse. If the pastness of racism requires sticking to the 'accepted meaning' of racism, it is also taken as licence to position racialized knowledge, artefacts and discourses as innocent-once-more, valid subjects of open debate and enquiry because *we* are all over race. Ironically, this position also constitutes a refusal of the closure it purportedly recommends. It advances a powerful assumption that the dominant repudiation of racism, narrowly under-stood, is sufficient grounds to recuperate racist ideas and genealogies as now nothing more than ideas, and thus contributions to open enquiry. While these tendencies appear contradictory, they are mutually reinforcing, and it is their convergence that informs the increasingly dangerous contention that anti-racism now represents a significant threat to freedom of speech.

The recent prominence of a discourse of 'viewpoint diversity', for example, explicitly lays claim to a consequentialist free speech heritage, whereby democratic health and human progress stem from a maximal exchange of opinion. This ostensibly pluralist ambition, however, seems disproportionately trained on questions of race. Reviewing the 'viewpoint diversity' website Heterodox Academy's original mission statement, 'The Problem', Carolyn Moxley Rouse notes how their main examples of 'questionable orthodoxies' arbitrarily excluded from ongoing rational evaluation are all about race:

> The list itself is revealing in that it aligns so closely with nineteenth- and twentieth-century natural sciences, which brought us polygenism, eugenics, and beliefs about the indelible connection among race, IQ, and behaviour. If Heterodox Academy were truly excavating academic orthodoxies, why not include in their list 'utilitarian economic theory', 'modernization theory', or 'American democracy'? Instead the authors

of 'The Problem' cast sociobiology, racist culture-of-poverty theories, and social prejudice as somehow falling victim to liberal orthodoxy. (2019: 175)

The narrow fixations of viewpoint diversity advocacy illustrate how racialized knowledge can be recuperated as an exercise in free thinking. Ideas that sought to shape human relations in the world, and have been politically repudiated in that world, are laundered as 'thought experiments' that increase the reasonable plurality of the public sphere. With racism repudiated and closure achieved on its meaning, everything can and should be open, and opened, again and again. All other forms of closure are represented as calcified orthodoxy, regardless of the histories and procedures through which these ideas, and their structures of legitimation, have been discredited. The idea of viewpoint diversity has little to say about what diversity encompasses in a context of discourse proliferation. More importantly, it depends on circulation without closure to repetitively restage the same debates. This same dependence produces the 'contrarian' as a recurrent speaking position in public. Consider one of the most successful such figures in Europe, Thilo Sarrazin, who carved out cultural space as an iconoclast even as he topped, in 2011, the German bestseller charts for twenty-one straight weeks with *Germany Abolishes Itself.* The book argues that Germany's essential, ethno-national identity is threatened by demographic factors, in particular the fecundity of 'Muslim migrants' and the 'mélange of other categories and factors that he suggests affect (their) intelligence and learning abilities ... including culture, gender, norms, religion, "incest" and "inherited disabilities" in ways that come close to asserting the innate inferiority of his subjects' (Meng 2015: 104).

As Michael Meng documents, despite this dependence on cultural and biological determinism in the service of social and ethno-national hierarchy, Sarrazin's critics were at pains to clarify that he was 'not racist', framing the book instead as an intervention into debates about the failure of integration. Sarrazin, on the other hand, sought out and pre-empted this 'accusation', presenting himself 'as a freedom-of-speech warrior who is cutting through decades of guilt-induced sidestepping' (Meng 2015: 131). Freedom of speech is invoked to prevent racial meaning being recalled to the problem of racism. Criticism of racist discourse becomes proof that the idea is *truly* too 'uncomfortable' to voice. Whereas the idea of the contrarian suggests a countervailing presence, probing a stifling horizon of consensus, the contemporary not-racist contrarian thrives precisely because of the speed and churn of media culture. The 'unorthodox' status of dismally familiar racialized ideas can only be laundered through circulation, through the renewal that comes with actively seeking out opportunities to be volubly 'silenced'.

The very idea of public debate exudes a glow of democratic potency, one that all too often remains undimmed by any reckoning with the barriers and inequalities to meaningful participation that shape public cultures. Postracialism burnishes this further, signalling an 'open debate' about the meaning of racism that is, in important ways, structured by the injurious contradictions explored in this chapter. Discussion of racism, we are told, has become too expansive, shutting down debate by erecting taboos and disciplining speech. Anti-racism is increasingly cast in the role of censor, granted exceptional powers to silence in a context of abundant, endless communication. And yet, in terms of public participation, anti-racism is a cluster of political tendencies and actions struggling, at minimum, for a meaningfully pluralistic public sphere. It does so at a moment when, however contingently, digital media platforms and networks provide modes not only of participating in public discourse, but also of questioning the terms on which it is conducted. It is amidst these tensions and contestations that the seemingly dry, objective question of definition has come to act as a disciplinary tool. If racism is historical, shifting in form and expression, then so are the ways in which it is denied. Postracial denial says you can talk about racism as much as you like, as long as it does not exceed the terms of a definition that we control. It is on this basis that the questions explored in the next chapter, of who is seen to truly practise – and truly value – free speech, take shape.

THREE

Culture: who values free speech?

Introduction

In 2016 the International Federation for Human Rights issued a report on the conduct of the state of emergency declared in France following the terrorist attacks in Paris in November 2015, attacks which had been preceded by the murderous assault on the offices of *Charlie Hebdo*, and a kosher supermarket, in early January. The état d'urgence, extended five times until it expired following the presidential elections in November 2017, granted the government extensive powers to ban public assemblies, close mosques, order house arrests and sanction police raids. Launching the report, a participating legal expert, Ramzi Kassem, recounted a story from a research interview with a Muslim man whose home in Paris had been subject to a raid:

> Armed, masked men burst in late at night without offering the occupants a chance to open the door,

training their weapons on adults and children alike. The agents made the homeowner lies face down on the floor, cuffed him, then searched him in a needlessly harsh, humiliating way. All of a sudden, they hauled the homeowner to his feet and pointed to a picture of a bearded man on his wall. 'Who is this bearded man?' barked a masked agent. 'Why sir', replied the homeowner, 'it's Victor Hugo.' (Kassem 2016)

The anecdote encapsulates the abusive failure documented in the federation's report: in the year of the study, over 3,500 raids resulted in just six 'terrorism-related inquiries'. It also, in its almost absurdist perfection, illustrates the force of suspicion brought to bear on Muslims and those taken for Muslims – particularly in deprived and repressively policed urban areas – in the febrile political atmosphere of 2015–16. How did the author of *Les Misérables* come to be misrecognized as a radical prophet for the wretched of the earth? In the immediate aftermath of the January attacks, the government of François Hollande emphasized the need to demonstrate national unity. Schools were a particular site of concentration, where the expression of this unity required reasserting 'Republican values' against the 'religiously inspired' barbarism of the attackers through a minute's silence, chains of solidarity, and discussions of the foundational value of *laïcité* (state-administered secularism). In the days following the attacks these expressions of unity were valued, rejected – a week after the attacks, for example, a significant group of intellectuals published an open letter in *Le Monde*, 'Non à l'union sacrée', rejecting the divisiveness of unity – and swiftly freighted with the suspicion we see concentrated, some months later, in the raiding agent's adventures in literary theory. In the press, stories began to circulate of young children and teenagers 'of migrant background' being questioned by police for allegedly refusing to respect the minute's silence or other gestures that represented, according to the education minister Najat Vallaud-Belkacem, 'too much questioning [that] came from pupils' (Marlière 2015).

This outbreak of what Philippe Marlière pointedly termed 'French McCarthyism' (2015) contrasted uneasily with the simultaneous emphasis on freedom of speech as a defining Republican value. 'The Republic', Hollande declared, 'equals freedom of expression.' The Prime Minister, Manuel Valls, went further, pronouncing that 'France carries freedom of speech everywhere.' Inevitably, given the extraordinary flow of discourse produced by these attacks, the hypocrisy of these declarations was immediately noted, for example in unfolding social media commentary on the enormous march of national communion on 11 January. If France equalled freedom of speech, how could its elected representatives march in Paris with world leaders responsible for imprisoning, torturing and killing journalists, political dissidents, bloggers and protestors? The charge of hypocrisy is accurate, but this accuracy notwithstanding, moral criticism has very little purchase if we accept that this march proceeded, in Mondal's metaphorical terms, through speech's jagged topography, rather than across the extensive surface of liberty.

In the aftermath of the January attacks – tellingly framed by *Le Monde* as France's 9/11 – the French government briskly replicated the signature claim of the 'war on terror' that curtailing civil liberties was necessary to preserve the freedom of 'our way of life'. As with the other sites of the nebulous 'war on terror', freedom of speech's cultural value was intensified even as speech – understood across its composite dimensions of press freedom, the right to protest, freedom of assembly – was made manifestly less free. This close identification of French nationhood with freedom of speech accompanied the widespread deployment of the 'apology for terrorism' provision in 2014's anti-terrorism bill against a vast range of loose or misreported pronouncements that could be seen as supporting terrorism.

These included drunken rants, psychiatric outbursts and random comments in school by children as young as eight (Hajjat 2017).

Katherine Gelber analysed the impact of post-9/11 counter-terrorism measures in the US, UK and Australia and noted their striking congruence with an enduring 'new normal' of constrained and criminalized political speech. She approaches freedom of speech as a 'principle and practice' that is mediated institutionally in a range of ways. It is a celebrated public principle, laden with 'ideational force' across these national contexts, but there are divergences in institutional procedures and speech practices. This attention to scales of action provides a way of approaching how, beyond the manifest hypocrisy, it is possible for political actors in these countries to invest rhetorically in the defence of freedom of speech even as they curtail it through political action (2019: 13–16).

This chapter argues for the need to probe the 'ideational force', or presumed universal power, of freedom of speech further. As a dominant political imaginary it cannot be fully understood without examining the racializing work it has, since the early 2000s, been pressed to perform. Claimed not just as a public principle but as an intrinsic value of the nation, respect for freedom of speech has been positioned as a threshold for evaluating the cultural compatibility of those racialized as non-European with the otherwise fully achieved ethos of the national community. Given the importance of liberal values to the articulation of contemporary nationalisms, free speech has become a pronounced dimension of the transnational obsession with Muslims as 'an overriding symbol of difference against which national identities are dressed and political agendas are set in the Western world' (Göle 2017: xvii).

The coordinates and intensities of this demand and obsession, as we shall see, differ contextually. Common to the transnational reproduction of the 'Muslim otherly mix' (Hage 2017a: 6), nevertheless, is that securitarian and cultural suspicions bleed into and sustain each other, and are given political force through the inter-action of state security, immigration and 'integration' structures and practices. Muslim Others, racialized as 'non-European' in colonial and orientalist imaginaries, are never quite of the nation. In the context of two decades of counter-terrorism, securitarian immigration politics and the relentless, mediatized production of a 'problem population' already within the gates, this relational positioning has been maintained by constantly seeking proof of capacity or willingness to respect the equality and freedoms integral to the nation. It is in this context, of relentless demands to demonstrate loyalty to a way of life, and compatibility with the values that are held to define that way of life, that freedom of speech has been loaded with further racialized contradictions. The next section examines how dominant approaches to counter-terrorism have fixed on speech by 'Muslims' as a source of suspicion and potential harm, requiring surveillance, restriction and intervention. The following section discusses the complementary cultural demands in this period, where respect for freedom of speech is projected as a primary marker of 'Muslims'' uncertain integratability, demanding evidence of their capacity to appreciate the corrective value of 'being offended'.

When they hear us

Despite the current vogue for declaring free speech crises, much contemporary commentary on free speech seems unwilling or incapable of integrating a consideration of how speech is distributed. Political freedom, material possibility and symbolic legitimacy organize the value of speech – who can speak, who can be heard and who is listened to.

There was an outbreak of freedom of speech anxiety in Australia in 2016 after a well-known cartoonist was briefly investigated by the Australian Human Rights Commission for a cartoon promulgating stereotypes of Indigenous Australians as irresponsible drunks. In their analysis of this, Bond et al. contrast powerful politicians suggesting the revision of hate speech provisions that threaten the 'right to be a bigot' with the expansively applied and disproportionately selective use of 'obscene language offences' in public to arrest and detain 'Blackfullas' in a system of incarceration notorious for the violent treatment of Aboriginal and Torres Strait Islander people. Who can speak? 'So long as some may exercise their right to be bigots, while others don't have the right to walk home, debates about free speech are futile' (2018: 422).

In 2019 the Kurdish Iranian writer Behrouz Boochani won several prestigious Australian literary awards for his book *No Friend but the Mountains*, awards he accepted via WhatsApp during his sixth year in 'offshore detention' on Manus Island in the Papua New Guinea archipelago. In Australia, as elsewhere in the 'west', the border is a system not a line, a technology of racialization. Australia's privatized network of punitive detention centres is designed to 'stop the boats', further weaken the legal right to claim asylum, and isolate people seeking asylum from networks of solidarity and publicity. Boochani spent close to five years writing his book on his phone, texting it in Farsi to be translated, and documenting, inter alia, the flourishing brutality of the detention centres. Who can be heard? Here he describes prisoners re-entering the camp after the intensely violent repression of an uprising in 2014, during which 23-year-old Reza Barati was killed:

> Alongside the walls of the tent enclosure/
> Bodies on top of bodies/
> A mixture of blood/
> Different blood flowing into each other/
> One blood/
> The sound of moaning/
> A crescendo/
> Different tones, different styles, different vocals /
> A war ballad /
> One bloodied mouth sings /
> Another bloodied mouth follows. (2018: loc. 4809)

On a hot summer day in July 2016, Adama Traoré, on his way to celebrate his birthday, fled from plain-clothes police in Beaumont-sur-Oise, north of Paris, as he had forgotten his ID. Some hours later he lay dead from asphyxiation in a police station courtyard. The death of yet another young man of Maghrebian or sub-Saharan African descent through 'contact' with the police sparked immediate protests and a movement for justice, centrally involving Adama's family, which was still demanding answers and organizing marches against police violence three years after his death and the discrediting of an initial autopsy and police accounts. The cost of this speaking out in public has been remorselessly extracted; the protest gatherings have been kettled and tear-gassed, the Traoré family's neighbourhood subject to police raids, a posthumous police investigation opened against Adama for 'resisting arrest', and the Mayor of Beaumont attempted to access town council funds to sue Adama's sister, Assa, for 'defamation' for claiming in an interview that the mayor 'is on the police's side, which means the side of police brutality' (Vigoreaux 2016). Who is listened to? Assa Traoré, noting that only one government minister had commented publicly on the case, and then to express support for the Mayor while avoiding any mention of her brother's name: 'I didn't think that justice was so vicious. If you don't look for the truth yourself, they won't help you' (Zeroula 2016).

These vignettes attest to how the question of what issues come to publicly constitute 'free speech crises' and which do not, and why, is absent from current debates. How certain forms of speech are rendered legible or illegible as speech that can aspire to be recognized as free speech is a problem which requires attending both to certain forms of speech, and to certain categories of speakers. In these three vignettes, freedom of speech is specifically constrained because the speech in question has been redefined, through political and legislative acts, as an *action subject to special control* – a public order offence, a question of state security, a matter of dignity in public office. It is speech shifted beyond the margins of liberty's homogeneous plane through political reclassification and an attendant mesh of institutional practices. It is also constrained, more fundamentally, because freedom of speech does not survive the violation or cancellation of rights through state violence for those systemically marked out as suspect, surplus or superfluous. The speech of those racially defined as subordinate in the settler colony, the postcolonial nation and the mutating border apparatus is 'silenced' by violence which kills, sequesters and breaks. Yet in a context of postracialism, it is presented as nothing more than a sequence of exceptional and regrettable acts in states otherwise fully committed to 'democratic values'.

This dynamic is vital to the transnational distribution of contemporary anti-Muslim racism, and understanding it requires recalling how the governmental value of values has been so central to the 'war on terror'. The post-9/11 invasions, as Derek Gregory (2004) noted, reinstantiated the 'split colonial geographies' of civilization and barbarism, giving compound force to a powerful reserve of essentialist knowledge about the 'Muslim world'. The bare-knuckle proposition of a 'clash of civilizations' stimulated the neoconservative world-making drive through its performative simplicity; a base–superstructure model where 'the politics of the Muslim world' is determined by the inherent violence of 'Islam'. Ultimately more powerful, however, was the gloved refinement of a 'clash *within* civilizations' (Kumar 2012) which promoted an interventionist governmentality based on cultivating the 'underde-veloped' – 'winning hearts and minds', bolstering 'moderate Islam', promoting civic development and gender equality – and killing and sequestering the 'undevelopable' (on these terms, see Weber 2015). The invasions of Afghanistan and Iraq, Tony Blair declared, were 'not just about changing regimes but changing the value systems governing the nations involved' (in Kundnani 2014: loc. 1099).

As Gelber documents, the 'war on terror', while conducted in the key of freedom, has had serious consequences for freedom of speech. The suspension of civil liberties and assault on human rights after 9/11 included severe speech-limiting provisions, redefini-tions and restrictions that largely remain in national legislations. In the United States, and subsequently the UK and Australia, for instance, definitions of 'providing support' for or 'advocating' terrorism were substantially expanded to encompass a broad range of political speech:

> In the USA, in spite of the constraints of the First Amendment, new provisions were introduced that criminally prohibit purely speech-based advice, even when that advice is designed to dissuade people from engaging in terrorism. In the UK, new criminal provisions prohibit the encouragement of terrorism based on a capacious conception of encouragement. In Australia, far reaching limitations on speech have been introduced, even where they have little or no connection to substantive terrorist threats. (Gelber 2019: 15)

This has been accompanied by expansive surveillance designed to pre-empt threats by amassing data from which it is assumed that profiles or patterns of risk can be discerned. Since the October 2001 USA Patriot Act granted broad powers for electronic surveillance and wire-tapping without a warrant, surveillance regimes in the US, Australia and the UK have expanded in scope and remit, particularly in relation to accessing Internet and phone data, while being subject to extensive legal challenges by civil liberties groups in this period. It is no coincidence that by six months after the Paris January attacks, all branches of the French legislature had approved a surveillance bill granting blanket surveillance and compelling Internet service providers to make data – such as browsing histories – available at the request of the intelligence agency (Toor 2015). Counter-terrorism, in other words, has been underwired by, while also boosting, the expansion in scope and powers of surveillance states that are constantly expanding capacities to extract 'predictive' personal data.

If counter-terrorism has constructed a punitive regime of surveillance and pre-emptive action, the political justification for this has required not just investing in the 'ideational force' of values under threat, but identifying the suspect populations these values must be protected from. This bleed from securitarian to culturalist rationales has been significantly advanced through the post-9/11 investment in theories of *radicalization*, further expanded by the counter-terrorism response to the 2005 London bombings, and seamlessly adopted in France after 2015 (see Plenel 2016). Clearly, government agencies should be trying to understand the causes of terroristic violence in order to pre-empt and combat its perpetrators. The problem, as Arun Kundnani (2014) has patiently demonstrated, is that operative radicalization models often begin from an exclusion or diminution of politics as an explanatory aspect of violence; instead, 'individual psychological or theological journeys, largely removed from social and political circumstances, are claimed to be the root cause of the radicalization process'. The result, he argues, excludes any consideration of the dynamic relation between state and non-state actors, fixing instead on a cultural solution, to engineer 'a broad cultural shift among Western Muslims while ignoring the ways in which Western states themselves have radicalized – have become more willing to use violence in a wider range of contexts' (2014: loc. 184). Radicalization thinking has promoted a paradigm of deterministic interpretation that loads any public demonstration of religiosity or radical political commitment by young Muslims, in particular, with 'extremist' potential.

The institutionalization of radicalization has resulted not only in political restrictions on speech through criminalizing legislation, but in a more diffused yet powerful set of restrictions, *on being heard* outside of the framework of 'extremism'. A substantial body of research has examined this erosion of the political through the various iterations of the Prevent Agenda in the UK, one of the four policy pillars of the CONTEST counter-terrorism strategy developed after the 2005 London attacks. Prevent's mission was set out as deterring 'those who facilitate terrorism and those who encourage others to become terrorists' while also 'engaging in the battle of ideas – challenging the ideologies that extremists believe can justify the use of violence' (Mottram 2008: 50). Prevent aims to tackle 'all forms of extremism'; in practice far-right violence has been generally treated as a 'public order problem' while the politics of deradicalization has extensively profiled Muslim communities (Sian 2017). These strategies depended on simulating a permanent state of emergency that 'securitised' civil society as a surveillance mechanism (Husband and Alam 2011). Crucially, this disproportionate security response was influenced by the thinking embedded in established 'community cohesion' frameworks that, particularly after riots in northern England in 2001, had institutionalized assumptions about 'Muslim communities' as leading 'parallel lives' at odds with the 'cultural norm'. Thus, while political rhetoric assured individual Muslims that they were a valued part of Britain's diversity, both rhetoric and practice assumed a vision of 'self-segregating communities' acting as incubators of religious and political extremism (for a detailed empirical refutation of these narratives of 'parallel communities', see Finney and Simpson 2009). Consequently, the message of Prevent was that Muslims 'must share a common burden of being targeted as legitimate objects of suspicion through the assertion that terrorist activity is being nurtured within their communities' (Husband and Alam 2011: 4).

The 2015 UK Counter-Terrorism and Security Bill extended and made compulsory Prevent reporting of potential signs of radicalization in all levels of education, in youth work and in health care. This statutory implementation was denounced in an open letter by a long list of academics arguing that Prevent's fixation on 'religious ideology as the primary driving factor for terrorism' is not evidence-based and thus inevitably leads to a 'focus on religious interaction and Islamic symbolism to assess radicalisation' (Lister et al. 2015). In Brown and Saeed's research with British Muslim women of Pakistani background studying in universities in England, they situate their experiences within the context of how Prevent's focus on 'religious ideology' as a driver of extremism renders Islamic symbolism, lifestyle or public commitments inherently suspect:

> As the processes involved remain undetermined, radicalization is frequently reduced to the profiling of traits or attributions of signs of radicalization in 'vulnerable' or 'at-risk' populations ... for example,

not living a 'British' lifestyle renders a Muslim (or community) disenfranchised or rebellious and therefore a suspect-radical ... consequently 'radicalization' encompasses a broad concern with a way of life rather than specific behaviours or actions, which has allowed for the securitization of ordinary or unexceptional lives. (2015: 2)

There is no dissent, just cultural indicators; when young British Muslims are cast as a population uniquely vulnerable to 'radicalization', the space for radical politics open to Muslim and non-white students is closed off (though Prevent, in theory, as the open letter argued, could be used against any form of anti-establishment politics on campus). The systemic suspicion legally required of university workers vis-à-vis Muslim-looking people poses once again the earlier question: what issues come to constitute a free speech crisis, and which do not, and why? It is not just that this constriction of political expression and assembly – one of freedom of speech's most foundational justifications – is not included in the delineation of crisis. It has been overshadowed by the attempt of some British Conservative party politicians and sympathetic media commentators to depict students as uniquely censorious, culminating in plans to censure universities that fail to stop 'no-platforming and safe spaces' shutting down 'legitimate free speech' (C. Turner 2018). A subsequent parliamentary cross-party investigation found, however, that 'press accounts of widespread suppression of free speech are clearly out of kilter with reality' (Busby 2018). The human rights organization Liberty was quick to draw out this juxtaposition, concluding that the 'government spuriously accusing today's students of threatening free speech' was a deliberate distraction from how Prevent 'imposes obligations on universities that either directly interfere with speech or have the foreseeable and actual effect of chilling the exercise of free expression' (Adams 2019).

Under radicalization's regime of interpretation, Victor Hugo's beard is all that matters; one cannot risk not taking ordinary signs as extremist wonders. And yet this regime persists, despite the body of evidence which shows how the biographies of successful terror attackers do not map onto model-based expectations, and the demonstrable inefficiency of mass surveillance in preventing deadly attacks. This illogic, Sharma and Nijjar suggest, is an outcome of the drive now institutionalized in the networked system of prevention. Constructing a heavily culturalized 'Muslim population' as suspect because of what is yet to materialize can only serve, systematically, to create further anxiety about what is unknown but may yet come. Thus, 'rather than only attempting (and inevitably failing) to identify real terrorists, a racialized surveillant assemblage resolves to *control* Muslim populations' (Sharma and Nijjar 2018: 82, emphasis in original); that is, populations assembled from historically racialized ethnic identities within the nation, unwanted mobilities at the border and, as the argument now examines, presumed signs of threatening difference in public space.

The right to offend

The 2015 attacks in France, Abdellali Hajjat notes, saw the increased circulation of the neologism *désolidari-sation*, a demand for Muslims in France to openly mark their non-solidarity with the stabbers, shooters and bombers. The demand for a collective response imputes collective implication or even guilt, but even more basically, it presumes a collective: 'So-called Muslims constitute a diverse population in terms of social class, nationality and political and ideological leanings, all of which is erased entirely by the call for *désolidarisation*' (Hajjat 2017: 81). In the more conspiratorial, identi-tarian articulation of this call, promoted by France's considerable cast of radical right public intellectuals, anything less proves that Muslims are a 'people within a people', bent on the destruction of an integral way of life. In a putatively more progressive iteration, marking non-solidarity demonstrates fidelity with a political way of life now under attack, thus requiring, according to the former Prime Minister Alain Juppé, 'that French Muslims clearly state that they have nothing to do with this fanaticism, this barbarism, that they fully subscribe to the values of the Republic' (Guénolé 2015).

Juppé's rhetoric may betray the emotional intensity of the moment, but his basic coordinates locate this demand in a wider politics of integration ascendant over the last fifteen to twenty years in western and northern Europe. Often superficially described as a form of 'civic integrationism', varying political projects in this period have pivoted on articulating the value, or at least reality, of lived diversity. This vision of the globalized, post-migration nation de-emphasizes the assumed cohesion of ethnic homogeneity in favour of cultivating a unifying liberal-democratic culture of shared values. This cultivation is not primarily focused on forming a pluralist public sphere where differences can be expressed; rather it is focused on governing public subjectivities and demanding evidence of the active acceptance of 'liberal values' as a condition of entry to and contingent membership of the 'national community'. The intensity with which gender equality, sexual freedom and free expression have been mobilized as defining of 'our' way of life as against the unsettling alterity of Muslims is a source of potent political confusion: how can it be 'racist' to insist that they integrate, and not threaten democratic life and egalitarian norms?

This tension between progressive rhetoric and coercive practice is less confusing if it is approached, as Elizabeth Povenelli (2011) argues in her discussion of what she terms 'late liberalism', as a form of *governmentality*, or management of population. Late liberalism, in this argument, is shaped through the mid-to-late-twentieth-century 'legitimacy crisis' generated by anticolonial and new social movements' challenge to inequality and ethnicized citizenship. One pronounced response to these challenges has been the reflexive creation of 'spaces within liberalism' for 'the recognition of difference', such as the plethora of initiatives and rhetorical visions often stuffed, inaccurately and exaggeratedly, into the capacious category of 'multiculturalism'. While, even across significantly divergent iterations in Europe, multiculturalism has very rarely amounted to more than a patchwork of initiatives and semiotic investments, the widely shared political narrative that it has gone too far and been too tolerant of excessive difference has provided, since the early 2000s, significant impetus to governmental rationales for assertive forms of integration (for comparative discussion see Lentin and Titley 2011).

This assertiveness reinvigorates a distinctly colonial relation, where freedom is animated, to return to Povinelli's description, as an 'imaginary of national and civilizational *tense*' (emphasis added). Integration demands that 'immigrant populations' demonstrate their capacities to embrace recognizable, 'future-oriented' social projects, organized around reforming 'backwardness' and emerging from 'pastness' through the apprehension of values. It is here, as Joe Turner summarizes, that 'apparently race-blind logics of temporality, freedom, commitment to LGBT rights and notions of "love" become means of distinguishing who has value in late liberalism' (2018: 773).

The articulation of societal cohesion has been increasingly vested in the specification of values simultaneously presented as universally valid and a national achievement, values, in other words, that it is perfectly reasonable to demand integration into. As Jan Dobbernak (2014) suggests in relation to the 'muscular liberalism of British values' articulated by David Cameron in 2011, such political projects are not 'stimulus-response models' determined by the actually existing social or religious conservatism of Muslims, or the active anti-liberalism of, say, particular, organized Islamist movements. 'Muscular liberalism' is not a political modality with a 'coherent and continuous orientation' but is rather mobilized to governmental ends, rhetorical effect and politically expedient goals, a 'display of sovereign assertiveness for which the implementation of liberal ideas offers nothing more and nothing less than a conduit' (2014: 15). Comparably, the post-2015 French drive linking national security to social cohesion, while narrated through a Republican emphasis on the historical achievements of secularism, is better understood as influenced by a very recent *néo-laïc* framework which has reshaped secularism around the fundamental problem of any and all displays of Muslim 'religiosity' in public space, read as evidence of their presumed cultural and religious 'communitarianism' and the threat it poses to the universal values institutionalized by the French state (see Mondon and Winter 2017).

Other national articulations have different priorities and narrative aspects, yet they converge, as Mouritsen et al. conclude in a comparative overview, on 'the securitisation of the (Muslim) other's uncivicness as something which cannot become included in the nation unless amended, and the concomitant emphasis on the receiving nation as a community of citizens, each contributing to its improvement as hard working, tax-paying, democratically competent and loyal' (2019: 644). The claim that 'liberal values' are definitive of the nation can only be secured by seeking out a defining contrast with the inherent religiosity, assertive patriarchy, risky transnationalism and brittle loyalties flatly held to characterize 'Muslim communities'.

This fragile dualism has arguably been most pronounced in the positing of gender equality and sexual freedom as established dimensions of a hegemonic national culture, pointedly contrasted with the – supposed – patriarchy and homophobia of non-white, non-western others. This not only suggests that homophobia, sexism and gender-based violence are alien to the west; it also ignores the perspectives and practices of various movements and struggles, particularly anti-racist feminists of colour already confronting reactionary politics in their social contexts (Boulila 2019). This kind of erasure underlines how the 'value of values' has not only informed the anxious, securitized governmentality of the last decades, but also animated resurgent nationalist expression, in which economic, cultural and political anxieties are tied uniquely to the presence of those who do not belong. What we might call 'liberal nationalism' is distinguished not by worry

about the ethnic homogeneity of the nation, but by
fretting about those who may be incapable or unwilling
of properly belonging:

> Those racialised denizens who fall outside the param-
> eters of a pre-given, automated body politic (i.e.
> the white ethnic majority seen as constitutive of
> the nation) are said to encounter liberal democracy
> from a position of want or lack, a liberal deficit that
> becomes particularly acute when mobilised vis-à-vis
> the problem that the contemporary Muslim poses to
> the civic state. In other words, racialised minorities are
> intuitively represented as having to learn and adopt
> these liberal principles that are definitive of the nation.
> The presupposed white citizen is instilled, by default,
> with a civic universalist ethos while the racialised
> citizen, first-generation and otherwise, acquires these
> qualities. (Valluvan 2019: 71)

The activism of integration politics has aimed at
tackling this deficit. If problematic cultural difference
is surmountable (in contradistinction to how it is
understood by ethno-nationalist essentialism), then
dis-integrating tendencies and practices can be trans-
formed through intervention. This rationale suffuses
the spate of manufactured symbolic controversies in
western Europe – focused on hijabs, burkas, minarets

and halal food – which have sought to promote inclusion through spectacular forms of prohibition and *exclusion*. Concomitantly, freedom 'in a national and civilizational tense' can only perceive deficits that appear to endure as evidence of incapacity or wilfulness. When France's Minister for Women's Rights Laurence Rossignol furthered the endless 'hijab debate' in 2016 by contending that 'there are women that have chosen [to wear headscarves], there were also American *nègres* who were for slavery', her openly racist analogy reveals how a headscarf worn in public can only constitute a lack, or worse, a refusal of autonomy and self-determination. This ambiguity is important, for while Muslims are frequently regarded as *too cultural* – reducing, as Claire Alexander argues, 'the richness, textures and diversities of Muslim lives to conveniently packaged and caricatured "dog whistle" emblems of what Islam "is"' (2017: 15) – religious identity is also approached as an idealist choice.

If who is of value can be adjudicated through the values they demonstrate, it is unsurprising that freedom of speech has been made integral to Europe's restless thresholds of integratability. In part this is predictable, as the articulation of 'core values' is assembled from aspirational inheritances variously described as 'national' or 'European'. Nevertheless, it is also a claim that has been forged through unsettling events that have infused the value of free speech with both civilizational distinction and particularly national intensities of identification. The messy aftermath of the 'Danish cartoons crisis', for example, has served to elevate freedom of speech as especially defining of Danish culture and national identity. Given the violence which simmered and erupted in the episodic and drawn-out unfolding of the crisis, that what Peter Hervik (2011) terms the 'collective memory' of the cartoons crisis is primarily about the threat to 'freedom of speech as a Danish freedom' may be understandable. The meaning of political events, nonetheless, can only be fixed through narrative work, and it is now often forgotten that while the right to publish of *Morgenavisen Jyllands Posten* was never in question, the political and symbolic meaning of the events was subject to considerable antagonism in Denmark, and beyond, even as they gathered pace.

When, in September 2005, *Morgenavisen Jyllands Posten*, one of the largest national papers, published images of the prophet Muhammad by twelve cartoonists, it was accompanied by a text which argued that the publication was a stand against a slide to self-censorship in deference to 'some Muslims' insisting on 'special consideration of their own religious feelings. This is incompatible with secular democracy and freedom of expression, where one has to be prepared to put up with scorn, mockery and ridicule.' Publication marks one narrative starting point, but for many journalistic and public critics of the publication, the story starts elsewhere, with the stated desire to provoke by the newspaper seen as the latest instance of its involvement in neo-nationalist, anti-immigration, 'values-based campaigning'. The cartoons were intended as a polarizing escalation, and thus it was the question of *the uses of speech which is free* (that is, conduct in the public sphere) which informed journalistic rejection of the terms of debate. As an editorial in the left-wing national daily *Information* pointed out, 'How damaging would it really be if we could not go on calling Muslims medieval fanatics who are a thousand years behind us? Or that we could not go on defining a world religion as a terror organization? Would self-censorship here constitute a disaster?' (in Meer and Mouritsen 2009: 351).

This is why Hervik, in tracing the history of the period, is at pains to demonstrate how establishing the 'collective memory' of the cartoons crisis required significant political labour, smoothing away the open antagonisms that contested the conduct of publishing, but not the right to publish. The keen adoption of *Jyllands Posten*'s 'campaigning' understanding of free speech by the government of Prime Minister Anders Fogh Rasmussen was critical in this regard, not only defending the constitutional right to publish, but also foregrounding 'mockery' as an emblem of the absolute status of freedom of speech in Denmark, and as evidence of how progress is achieved: 'What is fundamental in this case is that enlightened and free societies are more successful than un-enlightened non-free societies, exactly because some dare to provoke and criticize authorities, whether they are political or religious authorities' (quoted in Hervik 2011: 191).

A comparable nationalist sacralization was accelerated after the attacks on *Charlie Hebdo*, framing widely circulated cartoons from the paper not just as expressions that have the right to be published, but as expressions of Republican virtue that must be appreciated in civilizational terms. A murderous assault on media workers is an attack on freedom of the press, and the significance of the violence could have been framed politically in a number of ways; linked, for example, to the notable increase documented by Reporters without Borders in the political targeting of journalists by state and non-state forces in and also beyond conflict zones (Freedman 2017). Instead, the magazine's highly divisive satire was, like *Jyllands Posten*'s adventure in culture war, influentially hailed as an exquisite expression of the kind of European, 'Enlightenment' iconoclasm that robust traditions of free speech have inculcated, and which too many Muslims fail to understand, and must be taught to appreciate. In both cases, that is, it is political choices which dictated that defending media workers' right to publish would be subsumed to appropriating freedom of speech as a specifically European civilizational achievement.

There is something transparently opportunistic about the sonorous self-regard of this political rhetoric, a recourse to what Ghassan Hage memorably describes as a 'racialised strategy of phallic distinction' where 'Westerners "flash" to the racialised Muslims to say, "Look what we have and you haven't got. At best, yours is very small compared to ours"' (2017b: 260). And yet, in conclusion, it is important to linger on this 'activist' iteration of free speech's civilizational value. It is not irrelevant that both cartoon publishers saw themselves as self-consciously historical actors; *Charlie Hebdo* in a heroic tradition of French anti-clericalism, *Jyllands Posten*'s culture editor Flemming Rose situating the publication of the cartoons as standing up to totalitarianism and testing 'the boundaries of censorship in a time of war' (Battaglia 2006: 29). The right to 'mock, insult and ridicule' therefore constitutes a defence of free thought and secular universalism, pushing back against the irrationality and special pleading of faith-based identification and reactionary public religiosity. Muslims not only have no right not to be offended, but should recognize the tough love proffered by inclusive mockery as a *pedagogy of offence*.

In both stylizations, the neglect of power is the condition of this projection. The 'right to offend' is a meaningless formulation that trivializes the political language of rights. The 'freedom to criticize religion', which newspapers and other bearers of concentrated communicative power legally and substantively possess, is presented as a critical achievement without 'taking any account of what political uses are made of it, who is formulating the critique to what end, the typical social positions of the believers of this or that creed, or the political operations being deployed by the ruling class' (Ongün 2019). It is for this reason that an utterly hegemonic focus on Muslim 'integration' is presented as the equivalent of taking a stand against the nineteenth-century Catholic Church, or Stalinist totalitarianism. Without such heroic narratives, basing media spectacles on the insufficient modernity of 'migrant' popula-tions consistently subject to structural discrimination, state surveillance and full-throated civilizational racism appears somewhat less iconoclastic. Islamophobia is often presented, from elements of the political left as well as right, as a 'silencing' term that prevents the criticism of religion. What this neglects is that the troubling backwardness ascribed to Muslims is essentialized through the focus on religious ideas, as these are held to determine what and how *they* think.

This ontological over-determination shores up the pedagogy of offence. Offence, in the conceit of the enlightened transgressor, is the shock of the modern, the healing pain necessary for entry to liberal democratic participation. This idea of offence collapses everything from passing irritation to reflexive humiliation to politicized anger to hurt at the profane into a term culturally coded as proof of rational inadequacy – you can choose, as the common refrain has it, not to be offended. It also, quite deliberately, narrows the range of the political and the communicative, fixing all protest or rejection as theologically derived. Yet much of the Muslim-led protest against *Jyllands Posten* in Denmark, and the long-established criticisms of *Charlie Hebdo* in France, stressed how the publication of cartoons signifies in a chain of actions rather than merely as discrete texts, actions designed to solicit reactions that can be adjudicated for their degree of enlightenment. Accepting 'offence' is not a democratic characteristic but an integration indicator, hence so much of the peaceful protest and thoughtful criticism aimed at both publications being treated not as evidence of freedom of political expression in a thriving, antagonistic public sphere, but as insufficient fidelity to a defining characteristic of the nation.[4] The pedagogy of offence, therefore, has served to tauten the 'double bind' (Hajjat 2017) experienced by many Muslims, caught between the essentialist appropriation of faith by violent militants, and the essentialist circumscribing of correct, sufficiently modern reactions by civilizational enthusiasts. Pressed from both sides, the horizon of offence compresses the political space available to describe and contest the intersecting strands of contemporary anti-Muslim racism (Tyrer 2012).

The irony, therefore, is that a cultural politics nominally precipitated by a fear of 'self-censorship' has served to reinforce the mechanisms of self-policing and restricted expression that many Muslims have experienced in these decades of war without end and integration without acceptance. The call for *désolidarisation* stands as an extreme instance of how those racialized as 'Muslims' have had to endure constant pressure to navigate the political application of 'Good Muslim/Bad Muslim' taxonomies. Yassir Morsi, in a reflection on these pressures prior to appearing on an Australian news programme to discuss a terror attack, wonders how to negotiate how 'the content of who I am and what I wish to say is always dictated by the existing form of the conversation'. To speak about politics, he realizes, he must first say the right things, erase himself as a threat, be a 'good Muslim' to earn the chance to talk about racism. And yet,

> I tried to talk myself out of it. For I knew I had been socialised into recognizing a basic rule. This is about survival, not about telling a truth. The Muslim community does not want you to be heroic here, they just want to mitigate the backlash. This is about making sure that the following day a sister does not get her hijab ripped off her head. (2017: 480)

Morsi's reflections underline, like Eddo-Lodge's stylized refusal, that public debates are always shaped by social, political and media mechanisms that simultaneously privilege and constrain, amplify and mute. These consistently constrict how racism can be discussed. This lattice of informal restrictions has been worsened by a civilizational politics of free speech that has been content to mark out suspicious populations regardless of the cost of this to, inter alia, political freedom, democratic participation and meaningful plurality in the public sphere. And, as the next chapter considers, a morbid consequence of this integrationist preoccupation has been to gift 'free speech' as a force multiplier to political reactionaries only too happy to ventriloquize liberal values, the better to hollow them out.

FOUR

Capture: what is free speech being claimed for?

Free speech heroes

A strange chain of solidarity events unfurled across Europe and North America in the aftermath of the attacks on *Charlie Hebdo*, staged by actors not normally recognized for their championing of Enlightenment values. In February 2015, the youth wing of the *Perussuomalaiset* (True Finns) party announced plans to host a 'Muhammad cartoon competition' because the attacks 'once again show us the true nature of Islam' and 'the defence of freedom of speech concerns us all'. Two months later, the Pro-NRW party of Nordrhein-Westfalen organized a similar competition, 'Freedom instead of Islam'. Not long after, the 'first annual Muhammad Art Exhibition and Cartoon Contest' in Garland, Texas, organized by a group called the American Freedom Defense Initiative, made global headlines when two would-be attackers of the event were shot dead by police. The leader of the Dutch

Partij voor de Vrijheid (PVV, Party for Freedom), Geert
Wilders, had been a speaker at the Texas event, and
used his party's statutory public service broadcast access
to stage the exhibition on live television, explaining
that 'I do not broadcast the cartoons to provoke; I do
it because we have to show that we stand for freedom
of speech and that we never surrender to violence.
Freedom is our birth right.'

That these expressive acts of solidarity were explicitly
rejected by *Charlie Hebdo* journalists is of little consequence, as their blessing was not sought for events
whose form and design long precede the attacks, or
for a loudly stated allegiance to freedom of speech that
has become an increasingly prevalent dimension of
far-right discourse and activity. As chapter 1 discussed,
this 'weaponization' of free speech is transnationally
pronounced, and when it comes to the far right, it
would appear obvious that their normative slogan-
eering is manifestly at odds with the drive of the
nationalist and racist politics that lay claim to it. And
yet, as with the state authoritarianism discussed in the
previous chapter, the charge of hypocrisy does not help
to explain why this capture of free speech is so politically generative and transnationally prevalent, even as
its calculated duplicity hides in plain sight. The aim of
this chapter to examine why the capture of free speech

has proven so politically productive for variegated far-right actors, focusing not just on how far-right practices lay claim to it, but on the event forms and amplification structures that sustain its reproduction.

As the opening examples suggest, a prevailing trajectory of appropriation can be traced from the themes of the previous chapter, and developing this requires accounting for the diversity of political actors involved in the chain of cartoon events. For while they can properly be included in something called the 'far right', this is less a set category than a relational term. As Enzo Traverso argues, 'with the election of Donald Trump as the president of the United States, the rise of a new nationalist, populist, racist and xenophobic right has become a global phenomenon' (2019: 3). This is manifestly true, but this rise is frequently sensation-alized in narratives that, in reaching for the shadow of the 1930s, fail to account for the contingent successes and defeats that characterize the contemporary period. Moreover, such accounts pay insufficient attention to the heterogeneity of 'far-right' actors, genealogies and ideologies, and its implications for the forms of cooperation that are possible within national and transnational relations. This complexity, nonetheless, should not distract from the central question of the far right's racialized violence, manifested in physical attacks on the street and the relentless production of 'problem populations' in political and media discourse, and the threat this poses, in multiple ways, to those targeted as alien to or corrosive of the nation.

The capture of freedom of speech has an important function in the politics of the contemporary far right. One reason for this is that anti-Muslim racism facilitates connections to the conventional political spectrum, and also across the far right's heterogeneous field of ideological distinctions and political forms. In examining what he terms 'convergence on the right', where ostensibly centre-right and conservative parties have forged formal and informal alliances with the radical right, David Renton argues that this would not have been possible without the securitized and racialized integration and immigration politics of the 'war on terror', which changed 'the boundaries of normal politics. Countries which became inured to mass deportation (Britain), to indefinite states of emergency (France) or the widespread use of imprisonment without trial (the US) have found it easier to adopt other measures of racialised exclusion' (2019: loc. 305).

The far right, in this understanding, has not just hypocritically hijacked 'the value of values'; it has further radicalized its exclusionary force, exploiting the 'hierarchies of belonging' patterned out by the immigration apparatus and the politics of coercive inclusion to inject further urgency, conspiracy and pathology into the threats which menace the nation (Back et al. 2012). As Caterina Froio argues, radical right positioning within the mainstream public sphere and political system often 'induces the far right to adapt its nativist discourse to the available discursive opportunities that define belonging to – i.e. legitimate acceptance within – the national community' (2018). The sliding signifier of 'Muslim immigration' provides a basis for convergence across the political right in different contexts because this threat to border sovereignty and the national community can be contextually configured through, for example, Christian identitarianism (as forcefully articulated in Poland and Hungary, particularly during and after the post-2015 borders crisis), defence of the secular and/or liberal way of life, and the communal, cultural integrity of the welfare state (for example, in Denmark and Norway). While the radicalizing and exaggerating energies of far-right discourse imbue the threat of 'Muslim immigration' with conspiracy and the pathology of cultural decadence and collapse, it cannot be artificially dissociated from the wider political terrain on which it has scavenged and adapted.

Free speech plays an important modulating role within this discursive economy as 'Muslims' have been transnationally over-determined as its proven enemies. As the unwanted *Charlie Hebdo* tribute events demonstrate, freedom of speech provides a structure for intensified expression, imbuing any provocation with the status of fearless democratic action. Within this template for action, the reactionary mind can run wild; when Rasmus Paludan wanted to drum up support for his newly formed *Stram Kurs* (Hard Line) party in advance of the 2019 Danish elections, he intensified his staging of 'tributes to free speech', which involve publicly burning the Koran, sometime wrapped in slices of bacon or 'doused with the semen of Christian men'. Claiming principled defence of the right to speech also legitimates contact between electoral and movement actors; Wilders was invited to the Texas cartoon-in by the event organizers, the *Stop the Islamization of America* network, founded by the blogger Pamela Geller, and which has connections with supremacist groups (Pigott 2017).

While the civilizational horizon of anti-Muslim racism provides free speech posturing with a particular, heroic valence, far-right capture precedes this concentrated animus and extends beyond it. To rally under the banner of free speech is to invite others, beyond the particular details of the day, to recognize the principle at stake, and to either support what is right or contribute to the further erosion of rights. The capture of free speech aims to create space for racist speech as a beleaguered expression of liberty, and positions the dissemination of racist discourse as a contribution to democratic vitality. This is why the generation of free speech scandals is so productive for the far right, particularly under contemporary conditions of political fragmentation and media proliferation. In an intensification of the postracial paradox discussed in chapter 2, this spectacular politics also advances the truth value of racist discourse, pressing claims for the status of that speech as a 'taboo' truth, a truth rendered unfree by the official hegemony of anti-racism. The idea of *capture*, therefore, is intended to underline how the moral and instrumental values of freedom of speech are mobilized simultaneously: we have the right to speak, and we speak a truth rendered true by its silencing. Far-right capture is an attempt to harness the moral force of liberty's smooth surface in contexts profoundly shaped by speech's ruggedly complex topography.

Cultural racism and unfree truth

Public discussion of free speech, John Durham Peters argues, inevitably acquires a 'recursive character'.

104

Controversies which pivot on the meaning, validity or impact of speech become as much about the status of the principle itself as the primary substantive issue, such that 'it is often impossible to tell the debate from the meta-debate' (2008: 275). For the far right, the meta-debate leverages public space, the specific demands of their politics both obscured and enabled by tapping into freedom of speech's ideational force. This kind of strategic appeal to freedom of speech, by fascists and far-right nationalists, is not new. In the 1930s, Oswald Mosley's British Union of Fascists presented its paramilitary mobilization as necessary to protect their free speech from 'reds' (Smith 2020). US neo-Nazi groups have an established history of appealing to both the legal provisions and symbolic register of the US First Amendment to secure political space to organize in public (Bleich 2011). However, the idea of speaking under erasure has a particular bearing on the structure of the 'cultural racism' that, over the last fifty years, has come to be regarded as the 'ideological master frame' of the radical right (Rydgren 2005).

Since the 1950s, parties of fascist origin in Europe have incrementally reinvented themselves through renewed involvement in electoral politics. They have sought to distance themselves from the overtly hierarchical racisms deemed damagingly redolent of the fascist past via the adoption of a 'new right' discourse of cultural differentialism. The idea of 'cultural racism' is often misunderstood as marking a historical break with biological notions of racism, a reductive reading that misunderstands how race has always served to tie body to blood to behaviour. Race, as chapter 2 discussed, is an active process; in indexing shifting valences of fear and anxiety to black and brown bodies, it is produced through a dynamic sliding between visible appearance, supposed status and presumptive culture. The significance of this 'cultural turn', therefore, is the creative register culture provides for coded forms of racialization. It also sets out relations of speech, a structure of victimhood that obscures and inverts historical relations of domination. As Barker (1981) examines, racialized migration is held to threaten the 'natural' relation between territory, people and culture. Faced with uncontrolled numbers and irreducible difference, it is the 'natural' tendency of all humans to form groups, as everyone has a 'natural home' (an argument which has been forcefully rearticulated, of late, in forms of ecological racism). Given this 'sociobiological' tendency, it cannot be racist to want to preserve a way of life; it is the ordinary common sense of felt bonds and lived tradition.

As Barker noted, the key move of populist racism is to launder political discourse as unmediated, popular truth: 'the very existence of fears about damage to the unity of the nation is proof that the unity of the nation is being threatened' (1981: 17). In a trope markedly reanimated in the immigration politics of Brexit, 'ordinary fears' may be the discursive product of significant political and media labour, but they are invoked as nothing less than solid evidence of a given reality, mediated only by the faithful account of the truth-teller. Racism, in this articulation, can never be anything other than an attempt to silence because it accuses the people of bad faith: *you are saying that they do not say what they really mean.* Barker's work on 1970s Britain, Balibar and Wallerstein's (1991) discussion of 'neo-racism' in 1980s France, and Stolcke's (1995) delineation of a 'new rhetoric of exclusion' in the far-right electoral successes of early 1990s Austria and Switzerland complete a sequence of influential explorations of the ethno-pluralist 'racisms without race' that are determinedly contextual. Nevertheless it is possible to abstract these ideas heuristically, as over decades the logics of 'cultural racism' have been subject to extensive 'cross-national diffusion and adaptation' (Rydgren 2005). A 'not-racist' differentialism justified by its distance from a racist politics of hierarchy; culture understood in terms so determinist that cultural difference is effectively racialized; a discourse of 'ordinary fears' that denies racism through the simple truth that the people cannot be racist; immigration as a zero-sum game inevitably involving losses for us and gains for them – this is the flexible scaffolding for the capacious politics of 'anti-immigration' in subsequent decades.

A recent example from outside these established sites of far-right ideological labour illustrates this, while demonstrating the significance of free speech capture. The True Finns party, fresh from adventures in cartooning, contested the 2018 presidential election with a campaign predicated on defending free speech. This is a curious headline symbolic investment in a country consistently ranked near the top of the World Press Freedom Index and the 'Freedom House' civil liberties index, and requires some explanation. In keeping with international trends in the early 2000s, influential nationalist activists connected to the party and ancillary ultra-nationalist movements recognized the strategic importance of online communities not only as sites of movement-building, but also as spaces where political rationales can be honed prior to wider public rehearsal. Far from constituting 'echo chambers', these spaces act as discourse laboratories, assiduously analysing media coverage and generating narratives and talking points for countering the presumed hegemony of progressive, 'liberal' positions in public culture. Even as the racialized threat of 'non-western migrants' and 'Muslims' to the ethno-nation animated the party and associated movements, significant effort was invested in framing anti-immigration politics as nothing more than a 'scepticism of immigration' that is 'discursively insulated ... from the social stigmas of racism and xenophobia' (Pyrhönen 2012: 101).

The idea of immigration scepticism is an academic notion designed to describe anti-immigration attitudes that do not make reference to explicitly xenophobic or racist rationales. Appropriated and subjected to the alchemy of the discourse laboratory, it soon began appearing in the self-descriptions and political justifications of True Finns politicians. Once in circulation, the idea of 'immigration scepticism' was reproduced in Finnish political journalism's labelling of radical right actors, and, crucially, in their construction of the spectrum of admissible public opinion. 'Immigration scepticism' has evident roots in the trope of ordinary fears, and its conjuring of an image of unfairly maligned heterodoxy is an example of the euphemistic creativity through which discourses of cultural incompatibility are reproduced. The elaboration of cultural racism has been characterized by a 'language war over racial reference' where 'it is possible for social actors to defend themselves against accusations of racism, [while] engaging in racist practices at precisely the same moment as their disavowal' (Pitcher 2009: 14).

This 'war' has generated a durable and adaptable repertoire, but it is also enervated by the wider volatility, discussed in chapter 1, of racism's public meanings. Under these conditions, the gambit of the far right is to empty the idea of racism of any political purchase, to ensure that it is always subsumed to the meta-debate, primed as the trigger of patterned controversies where the 'accusation' becomes as controversial as the substantive issue. Addressing a May 2018 'Defend Our Freedom of Speech' rally in London, called after he was banned from Twitter for repeated violations of its 'community standards', the former leader of the English Defence League 'Tommy Robinson' (real name Stephen Yaxley-Lennon) contended that 'the people of this country have been silenced for 20–30 years with the tag of racists', and hailed the rally as the beginning of the end of anti-racist censoriousness: 'They now realise that the tag is dead, no one cares anymore with being labelled racists' (Gayle 2018).

If freedom of speech is invoked to prevent racial-izing discourse being recalled to the problem of racism, what Robinson's contention illustrates is how it simul-taneously confirms the inverted relations of resentful nationalist victimhood. The veracity of ordinary fears cannot be secured without the threat of silencing, taboos cannot be broken unless vested interests attempt to enforce them, and uncomfortable truths have no truth effect unless spoken under erasure. The imagined relations of precarious speech have always required the shadow of anti-racist censoriousness, reducing a wide and fractious milieu of political tendencies to a singularly elite and therefore anti-democratic imposition. The right-wing bogey of the 'race relations industry' in 1980s Britain, for example, appropriated an autonomous anti-racist critique of cooption by state-funded bodies to posit anti-racism *tout court* as a powerful official hegemony that 'brings race into everything'.

Similarly, while formulaic and moralized language politics certainly exists, the transatlantic story, since the 1990s, of the imposition of political correctness is primarily a self-confirming fable. It allows conventional reactionary talking points to be renewed as common-sense dissent from a periodically declared 'new intolerance'. For all their appeals to plain speaking, the radical right are committed to language games, and this patterning of stylized responses has long been integral to what Ruth Wodak has termed right-wing discourse's 'perpetuum mobile' (2015: 19–20). But language games are not, as is so often assumed, superficial, and an effect of the decades of ideological and media labour poured into these holding positions is that the very mention of racism is now often regarded as that which primarily stokes division.

This is the presumptive purchase of free speech campaigning for the True Finns. In the demotic ventriloquism of radical right populism, where ordinary anxieties must be voiced by political leaders because normal people are not free to say what they are thinking, any political opposition can be mythologized as an apparatus of denial. It is frequently pointed out in contemporary public discourse that when 'populists' claim that their speech has been infringed they are mistaking criticism for censure, but this is less civic failure than political desire. Speaking under threat of erasure is the grammar of nationalist resentment; the authenticity and truth of what is said are an effect of who is attempting to silence it. Speech that is free is speech free of opposition, and yet the perpetual machine is oiled by criticism and charged by resentment; it is nothing without its critics.

This is, to use the phrase, a political 'playbook' of practised moves and ritual provocations, but its powerful contemporary resonances, Wendy Brown argues, owe much to the ways in which the rancorous resentment mobilized by the contemporary radical right is organized around 'novel iterations and expressions of freedom' (2018: 61). The volatile politics following the global economic crisis, shaped by neoliberalism's crash and state-enforced resurrection, converge on freedom as the driving force of 'manifestly unemancipatory' forms of authoritarianism and nationalist backlash. The effect of 'neoliberal reason' has been to cast the social as a fiction and the political as restriction, with the effect of discrediting 'norms and practices of inclusion, pluralism, tolerance and equality across the board'. The nationalisms that promise renewal in societies fractured by 'eroded socio-economic status and new forms of insecurity' can rail against globalization, but can promise no more than revenge against its racialized ciphers. This is 'taking back control' from those that do not belong and demand too much, and from those 'citizens of anywhere' whose urbane, cosmopolitan habitus promotes a multicultural politics tolerant of everything other than the legitimate concerns of those who truly belong. Ignoring the affective power of nationalist resentment, Brown argues,

> misses the extent to which the displacement suffered by whites, and especially white men, is not mainly experienced as economic decline but as lost entitlement to politically, socially and economically reproduced

supremacism and why, therefore, right-wing and pluto-
cratic politicians can get away with doing nothing
substantive for constituencies as long as they verbally
anoint their wounds with anti-immigrant, anti-Black
and anti-globalization rhetoric, and as long as they
realign the figure and voice of the nation with the
figure and voice of nativism. (2019: 69)

In the present moment, the freedom in freedom of
speech is also suffused with this desire to bridle at any
'arbitrary' restraint. And, with speech positioned as an
endangered civilizational property, any racist practice
can be presented for recuperation as a principled stand.
What Philomena Essed (Essed and Muhr 2018) has
termed 'entitlement racism' pivots on this relation
between 'an insistence on the right to offend in the
name of freedom' and a desire to humiliate, to be
allowed to enjoy racism without inhibition. Thus
'blackface' rituals can be justified as nothing more than
postracial innocence, but also an exercise in taking our
culture back; racist humour is nothing more than a
desire to increase the realm of expression, and yet it is
remarkable how consistently race provides the inspi-
ration for edgy 'thought experiments'; 'speaking one's
mind freely' remains comfortably shackled to racism as
a primary threshold of liberation.

The radical right has been quick to recognize this distemper. While 'dogwhistle' racism has been historically necessary to mark distance from the explicit racism of fascism, in this affective storm more overt attacks are openly licensed by the prerogative for speech to be free and the truth to be heard. Anything that is said in the interest of the people is legitimate, a licence which explains the increasing prevalence of far-right conspiracies about 'cultural Marxist domination' and the 'great replacement' of native European populations, bleeding into the recalibrated rhetoric of those centre-right actors who have converged with their radical outliers. And content, of course, is inseparable from form. Racist 'populist' discourse is an exercise in occupying political space, a gestural and spectacular politics designed to exhaust fact-checking and rational argumentation, a sustained exercise in signalling an organic connection to the 'authentic' people by repeatedly breaking the same never-quite-taboos, and cultivating the truth effect of outrage expressed by the 'elite'. Under these conditions, freedom of speech has been retooled as a technology of racist amplification, and the challenge for those that oppose the far right is how to navigate the disorienting meta-debate that they have succeeded in inducing.

Free speech events

What does it mean to speak of a free speech *event*, as opposed to incident, controversy or injustice? This argument has repeatedly drawn attention to the ways in which some issues become represented as free speech issues, and others, regardless of the extent of restriction or oppression involved, cannot lay claim to this form of public recognition. The regularity with which the politics of racism become subject to these quasi-ritual-istic controversies suggests that the patterning of these events is worth examining.

In *Courting the Abyss*, John Durham Peters notes how a 'threefold drama of the liberal enabler, the convention-buster, and the outraged bystander' provides a basic grammar for free speech events (2005: 8). The unfolding of the drama goes something like this. An 'outrage artist' breaks, in the name of freedom or progress, what they proclaim to be a taboo. Deemed transgressive, the act seeks support from 'friends of liberty', who can be 'wonderfully ingenious in interpreting offensive practices as defensible contribu-tions to public life'. However, the drama requires the third party, the 'offended' who fail to appreciate the inalienable freedom of the former, and the disinterested commitment to the common good of the latter. As with the relations established through the pedagogy of offence, in the free speech event, the most significant scrutiny often falls on the triangulating, offended party, those that become the story by seeming to reject freedom of speech's ideational force.

This account of recurring dynamics is not to suggest that all controversies concerning freedom of speech straightforwardly reproduce this template, or that when they do, these ritualized features fully determine the meaning of events. The chain of attempted cartoon competitions were textbook attempts to stage precisely this threefold drama, to create space for anti-Muslim racism by planning events designed to provoke conflict and thus to tap into the rich seam of principled meta-debate the dramatic structure promises. Nevertheless, fidelity to the template does not guarantee success, for with the exception of Wilders' intervention, these competitions fizzled out for lack of wider interest. Far more successful in mobilizing the triangulating dynamics of a free speech event has been the strategy of staging speaking events for high-profile racists on university campuses, goading opposition to disrespect their right to speak in a context dedicated to the pursuit of knowledge, and thus tapping potently into freedom of speech's ideational force. This force is particularly pronounced with respect to the cultural status of the First Amendment in the United States, and in recent years it has been tapped most spectacularly by the Internet-enabled white nationalist movements that convinced far too many media commentators to accept their rebranded status as the 'Alt-Right'.

Examining the attempts of the white supremacist Richard Spencer to organize lecture tours on US university campuses, Joan W. Scott notes the transparency of the desire for spectacle, where 'free speech means the right to one's opinion, however unfounded, however ungrounded, and it extends to every venue, every institution' (2017: 4). The freedom being claimed is liberty not from regulation but from any restraint on, *or refusal of*, engagement. The appeal to freedom of speech, in this calculation, means demanding that all contentions are treated as discrete goods in the marketplace of ideas; racial science, 'race realism', revisionist histories and even more brazen ideological set pieces are presented as arbitrarily stigmatized contributions to 'diversity of thought'. For the far right, this laundering of racist thought is a two-way bet. Engagement amplifies 'ideas' that have often sought pseudo-intellectual plausibility in symbolically significant settings; refusal provides publicized victimhood and suggests that opponents must resort to anti-democratic means because they are incapable of 'defeating' their arguments. 'Jews will not replace us', as the Alt-Right chant goes, and you will have to debate us.

The gaming of debate is one of many tactics honed through a significant political economy of reactionary front groups and think tanks that have, over decades, sought to intervene politically in US campuses – particularly public universities – by relentlessly framing them as sites of active indoctrination in 'liberal' ideology. As Isaac Kamola has documented, one trajectory of attack is determinedly anti-free speech, attacking academics involved in critical race or postcolonial studies, or active in anti-racism, or – more recently – the Boycott, Divestment, Sanctions (BDS) strategy against the Israeli occupation of Palestine. These attacks follow a 'common script' whereby 'a right-wing group captures something said, posted or tweeted by a faculty member, these statements are then decontextualized and wrapped in moral outrage, broadcast through the right-wing media ecosystem, and eventually find their way into the "mainstream" media' (2019: 3).

Targeting academics for harassment and career destruction is accompanied by extremely well-funded conservative and far-right-adjacent front groups – such as the tellingly titled Foundation for the Marketplace of Ideas – that attempt to stage speaking tours and

119

campus debates for figures, like Spencer, guaranteed to mobilize opposition and amplify spectacle. Despite the manifestly coordinated staging of free speech events, this cluster of actions, Joshua Clover argues, has largely been presented in the US press as a series of 'controversies' rather than as pivotal to the white nationalist movement's strategy of spectacular disruption. Thus, 'the world begins anew every day. Each further provocation is treated as without history and thus presumptively legitimate' (Clover 2017). Conversely, student and anti-fascist protests are treated as evidence of a deeper malaise, the – generationally renewed – incapacity of students to understand the higher commitments that, the story goes, bond fascists and those they target as illegitimate life forms in a shared, otherwise democratic community. In the predictable triangulation of the event, therefore, the problem becomes the attitudes and behaviour of the offended. Minouche Shafik (2018) provides an indicative version of this argument;

> Some would argue that we need to preserve universities as 'safe spaces' that shield young people from offensive ideas. But I believe that universities should provide spaces for the civilized contestation of ideas. Bubbles where the like-minded reinforce their prejudices are dangerous for open societies, which depend upon the

clash of ideas. We need to provide a forum in which those clashes occur productively to advance human knowledge.

This focus on the normative value of intellectual exchange, in isolation from any reckoning with the material impact and predictable content of the far-right debate industry, recalls the discussion in chapter 2 of the consequentialist tendency to idealize debate outside of the conditions and relations which shape it. In some variations this argument is tilted towards a political evaluation, maintaining that 'the freewheeling fight of opinions is the best insurance against a victory of inhumane ideologues' (Bittner 2019). However, in arguments drawing heavily on the influential metaphor of the marketplace of ideas, or on the *moral* status of the First Amendment, an ethics of abstention from judgement places its faith in the power of ideas to arrive at the true and the fair. That it is assertions as to the sub-humanity or implacable cultural alterity of historically racialized populations that endlessly demand open competition with other ideas does not merit pause for reflection, as what is at stake is a transcendent commitment, a wider ethics of civic tolerance. Peters has memorably termed this an attitude of 'homeopathic machismo', the conviction that doses of 'bad speech' provide the opportunity to respond with the kind of fortitude which girders democratic health, thus demanding an active practice of tolerance, agnosticism and civility from those committed to speech's foundational value (2005).

Without understanding the influence of procedural even-handedness as civic virtue, it is difficult to grasp the force with which the triangulating drama of the free speech event comes to focus on the problem of the 'offended', on those who block, refuse and de-platform. Leaving aside the somewhat unsettling obsessiveness with which a tiny handful of largely misreported events on US campuses have come to preoccupy generationally incurious US op-ed writers, this is the normative content of the 'snowflake' mythology. For the far right, the censoriousness of anti-racism licenses total disinhibition under the sign of freedom. For the 'friends of liberty', the problem of protestors' civic fragility and intolerance has the effect of imbuing the formal expression of 'offensive speech' – a designation which already strips it of ideological content – with democratic prerogative.

Consequently, democratic values, and the values of the university, require treating far-right ideology as a set of contentious ideas to be engaged with through *counter-speech*. While this position is regularly articulated in these conflicts in the United States, it is also transnationally pronounced. The rector of Bergen University has suggested that, given the need to correct the extent to which 'incorrect political views are being excluded from university discussions', it would be 'legitimate to invite Holocaust deniers to join in discussion' (Myklebust 2019). The Vice-Chancellor of the University of Auckland refused to have white supremacist posters removed from campus because 'there is a balancing act – and it is particularly important at a university – between the rights of the people to free speech and the rights of people not to be upset by things' (Meech 2019). These instances are telling, as they demonstrate how even the genocidal racism that forms the kernel of 'frozen' racism can become the subject of 'open debate' by being presented as a necessary intensification of the homeopathic remedy.

There are many points of entry to a critique of this position, not the least of which is the apparent indifference to historical and political knowledge suggested by the conceit that practised, motivated and closed forms of far-right discourse are amenable to reasoned engagement in the 'realm of ideas'. But this indifference is a symptom of a wider refusal to acknowledge that what is at stake in these controversies is not the self-affirming mythology of subjective fragility versus civic vigour. Instead, what is in play, most basically, is the antagonistic character of politics, and conflict between visions that do not share precepts about the political, the character of speech and the nature of communication. For example, opposition to far-right speakers is based on a rejection of the idea that racializing discourse should be treated as debatable in societies and contexts where it acts in and on the lives of its targets. Since racializing discourse covers a wide spectrum, from engaging in overt hate speech to the simulated intellectualism of 'revisionist' histories, strategies of protest have long been the subject of collaborative reflection, argument and adaptation. Liberal event triangulation simply ignores this intellectual and political heritage and treats the fact that anti-racist and anti-fascist politics do not proceed from its individualistic and idealist precepts as reason enough for summary dismissal.

Here, once again, the smooth surface of liberty is secured simply by refusing to recognize topographical features even as they loom resolutely into view. This is most evident in the confusion of freedom of speech with academic freedom, which, as Robert Post (2013) demonstrates, is not merely an extension of the former into the space of the university. The mission of the university includes discriminating between ideas on the basis of disciplinary norms and intellectual expertise, and foregrounding some ideas while actively neglecting those which have been discredited and disproven. This amounts to a qualitatively different set of communicative norms that 'contradicts the egalitarian tolerance that defines the marketplace of ideas paradigm of the First Amendment' (Post 2013: vii). This discrimination remains consonant with liberalism, nonetheless, for if there is a democratic entitlement not just to freedom of speech but also to the information and knowledge necessary to make informed decisions, then the specialized institutions this requires are not merely extensions of the public sphere. Therefore 'it is no intrinsic affront to the intellectual culture of the university ... that a person should be deprived of a platform to express her views because of a negative appraisal of her credibility or the content of her views' (Simpson and Srinivasan 2019: 206).

This argument is useful in confronting the 'intellectual racism' gathered around myriad attempts to reassert the scientific status of race (Saini 2019), which has always sought to present its debunking as an arbitrary restriction on academic freedom. It also explains why far-right-adjacent configurations such as the so-called 'intellectual dark web' are so keen to cast their YouTube-enabled business model as nothing more than a commitment to the 'diversity of opinion' that universities now 'repress'. Nonetheless, a reliance on the closure afforded by academic freedom neglects, as Nick Riemer argues, that the term 'does not refer to a singular right uniformly and indiscriminately available to everyone engaged in academic work [but is instead a] scarce and contested resource over which differing counter-communities compete' (forthcoming).

The university is not populated by a homogenous and consensual 'academic community' but is a site of competing and often antagonistic interests, and an institutional space where free speech, regardless of the prevailing universalist framing, is also unevenly distributed. The protests of racialized students and their allies insist on this as a starting point. Treating motivated ideological discourse that is predicated on invalidating the humanity of some members of the 'university community' as a formal contribution to the public good is to restrict not only their speech, but also their agency and security on campus. To insist that students who experience the consequences of racist politics sublimate themselves to an ideal community of discourse with white nationalist actors – who consistently clarify what the students' status would be in *their* ideal society – is a form of performative conscription. Event triangulation demands that students act against their safety and interests to bring into being the neutral

126

terrain of free speech that has never existed. There is no 'slippery slope', for as Angela Mitropoulos points out, this metaphorical appeal 'leverages a routinely unrealized anticipation that "free speech" *might* protect the "most vulnerable and marginalized in society" into repeated, *actual* instances of the defence of fascist speech in the present' (2017).

The weakness of the arguments portending free speech catastrophe in the United States is that they can only see protest as a rejection of counter-speech rather than, as with Eddo-Lodge's refusal to engage with the repetition of postracial sureties, a necessary condition for thinking about what meaningful dialogue could look like. This is nowhere more pronounced than in the dangerous equivalence frequently drawn between the authoritarian desire of fascist speakers and the 'student totalitarianism' that disrupts their platforms. As Evan Smith (2020) has shown in his study of 'no platforming', the now transatlantic term has an established twentieth-century history as a practice in British anti-fascism. Its prevalence as a specific political term owes much to the policies of the National Union of Students in Britain in the 1970s, which sought to counter intimidation and attempted organizing by the National Front on university campuses. Key here is the understanding that because fascist speech is action oriented towards furthering a violent politics of domination, there is no possibility of democratic debate. Instead, all forms of fascist activity constitute attempts at mobilization which must be defeated before they achieve traction.

When anti-fascist activists in the United States organized to prevent Richard Spencer speaking on campuses in 2015–16, very similar arguments were made. To take two prominent interpreters of 'antifa' tactics: 'Liberal appeals to Truth will not break through to a fascist epistemology of power and domination – these are Spencer and his ilk's first principles' (Lennard 2019: loc. 220); thus, 'Instead of privileging allegedly "neutral" universal rights, anti-fascists prioritize the political project of destroying fascism and protecting the vulnerable regardless of whether their actions are considered violations of the free speech of fascists or not' (Bray 2017: 144).

This debate does not apply only to fascists, however, and there is nothing to be gained politically or analytically by over-extending the term to reductively encompass a complex assemblage of racist political orientations. As Evan Smith (2020) demonstrates, some of the most significant political differences within left and anti-racist movements in the UK during the 1970s and 1980s hinged on whether no platforming was a tactic solely directed at the threat of organized fascism on campus, or whether it could be legitimately extended to racist, sexist and homophobic speech that contributed to conditions of harassment and exclusion in the university. In a history of campus free speech controversies in the Trump era, P. E. Moskowitz documents comparable disagreement among anti-racist students in Middlebury College as they debated whether to 'no platform' the author of *The Bell Curve*, Charles Murray. His repeated invitations to speak on campus suggested to students of colour that their demand for the university to oppose attempts to rehabilitate racial science was deemed less pressing than 'presenting racist ideas as worthy of debate'. Thus for the students 'the talk was not about a scientist presenting controversial findings, but about a racist who had deeply and materially influenced American policy, and who was at no risk of being silenced if he were not to speak at Middlebury – he was one of the most popular conservatives of the day' (2019: 50).

Disagreement as to what constitutes silencing marks the final significant line of tension between the 'enablers' and the 'offended' in the free speech event. As chapter 2 noted, liberal free speech theory often assimilates speech to thought, a move which configures speech as 'costless and priceless', that is, as of intrinsic value as an expression of conscience, but of no causal impact as an action in the world (Gelber and Brison 2019). Thus, to be denied an opportunity to speak offends freedom of speech because speech is an expression of autonomous thought. Varied forms of anti-racist refusal dispute this, pointing to the repetitive redundancy of far-right discourse, its patterned obsessions and discursive predictability. While universities anyway tend to invite high-profile speakers based on the publicity their ideas have already attracted, the 'talking point' structure of far-right discourse underlines that one does not have to hear it expressed to know what will be said. If, as James Carey argues (1992), two alternative conceptions of communication have dominated in American culture since the nineteenth century, free speech theory tends to prefer the dominant iteration, communication as the transmission of information and ideas. Yet the 'ritual view of communication' emphasizes the relations communication establishes and the contexts in which it *acts*. Far-right discourse plays on this distinction; it recognizes that speech is not just about communication, and seeks to ritually occupy space and attention while claiming that the transmission value of its arguments is unfairly dismissed.

No platforming tactics recognize that, when faced with the ritual power of closed discourse, with the repeated assertion of the problem that 'problem populations' present, blocking is a form of counter-speech. 'Speech acts', Rae Langton argues, 'can build unjust norms and authority patterns, helped along by hearers who do not block them' (2018: 146). To block is not to stem the transmission of ideas, but to stymie the cumulative force of ritual, drawing attention to the conditions of reception required for racism's successful reproduction. To refuse to play the roles allotted by the ritual is to refuse the postracial licence increasingly accorded to racializing discourse under the sign of civil debate.

Nonetheless, no platforming is a strategy, not a position. It recognizes that protest cannot fully unsettle the generative dynamics of a free speech event, and can rarely puncture the claim of victimhood that de-platformed speakers are usually only too happy to parlay into political and media currency. And it is also clear that in a digital multi-platform environment, which proliferates at pace and without end the talking points, memes and affective rhetoric of the far right, strategies of blocking and disruption are inadequate in a media ecology structured by the competition for attention. The Internet has been profoundly productive for the 'polymorphous galaxy' of the far right (Mammone et al. 2013), its informational architecture providing structural opportunities for 'information laundering' and disinformation (Klein 2012). Social media platforms, more recently, have provided organized movements with the opportunity to mobilize, troll and insert themselves into the news cycle. Increasingly they provide a scaffolding for a rapidly evolving media scene, comprised of punditry, political celebrity and entrepreneurial media ventures. In this environment, the appropriation of freedom of speech is a structuring dimension. Far-right 'news', conspiracy building and journalistic activism are shaped, all the way down, by the conceit of revealing hidden truths repressed by the mainstream: if our story or perspective does not appear in the mainstream, it is because it has been repressed by the elite, or liberal media. Everything is true because it has already been denied. The problem of capture is only beginning to take shape.

So, is free speech racist?

The titular question of this book can be answered in different ways, and posed in different ways also. In one version, it ventriloquizes the gleeful injury of the tendencies discussed in chapter 2 through the notion of capture: 'what, so even free speech is racist now?' The affective victimhood of nationalism fixes on racist speech as a marker of organic community, primed to lament at the first sign of disagreement: 'see, you can't say what you want in your own country any more'. The disciplinary tendencies of postracialism search out discursive excesses on Twitter and rush to proclaim, again, the death of the public sphere: 'I told you so, the accusation of racism is everywhere, all the time, shutting down public debate.' The wearying contrarianism of failing media business models recycles its uncomfortable truths about 'problem populations', praying for responses – any response will do – that can be parlayed into evidence of the tyranny of political correctness. Freedom of speech, in these recurring spectacles and punctuated declarations of crisis, is invoked not to alert us to political repression, material constriction or arbitrary violence. Rather, it is appropriated to attempts to restore authority, deflect criticism, compete for attention and, most forcefully, create space for racist expression. For those more interested in the value of free speech than the politics of racism, I have tried to demonstrate that the extent of this appropriation should nevertheless be of concern: delinked from dissent and human flourishing, it reduces freedom of speech to a reactionary banality of media culture.

For others, perhaps more concerned with understanding contemporary racisms, we can approach these investments in free speech as attempts to dictate the terms of communication and participation in diversified publics, while refusing the reality of their formation. The tendency to insist on idealized visions of public debate, blind to the jagged topography of 'actually existing' speech politics and conditions, is a critical expression of this. Freedom of speech has become increasingly regarded as the primary guarantee of 'public conversation': maintaining a free flow of ideas, investing all ideas with deliberative potential, and restoring a cohesion that was always an imagined or imposed dimension of public spheres. The extent to which securing this vision would depend on disciplining and excluding those who refuse its codes and procedures should demonstrate why it will never amount to more than a driver of antagonism. 'The universal', as Judith Butler points out, will never be restored through the 'fiat' of either demands for more and better rationality, or 'racially cleansed' projections of the 'common good' (1998: 36).

The central thematic arguments in this book examine how this assumed universality continues to legitimize and extend racializing processes and dynamics. When claimed as a property of the nation, freedom of speech works to shape who can speak, in what role and register, and how they will be heard and listened to. When understood not just as a commitment to freedom but as a virtuous disregard for how communication works and how meaning is made, it provides productive force to the articulation and reshaping of racist discourse. When lifted out of the racialized relations of the nation and system of borders, it delinks the liberty to speak from the freedom to act, live, survive.

Moreover, it seems clear that free speech has been invested with this intensive, totemic promise under communicative conditions that, in fact, require us to think profoundly as to what it now encompasses. The political and cultural consequences of an altered media and informational ecology are now a matter of urgent speculation. This must include reckoning with how speech is now an automated artefact, a machinic output produced and circulated independent of speaking subjects, a commodity maximized for profit by private interests providing a quasi-public, practically unaccountable transnational infrastructure. The expansive growth of communications, the sheer cluttering of personal experiences and social environments by incessant 'speech', suggests that political control is potentially exercised not just through suppression but also through proliferation, through the splintering of collectively oriented thought, the crowding out of shared reflection and the diminishment of relations of listening and hearing. There is a democratic project at stake here more encompassing than the arguments of this book, which involves thinking through the assumed relation of freedom of speech to human autonomy, collective flourishing, and political critique and action under conditions of informational abundance, media amplification and narrative multiplication.

The arguments herein intersect with this project, nonetheless, in rejecting postracialism's coercive dynamics of radical openness and arbitrary closure. Those who act in the face of racism do not need me to tell them when it is worth responding or not in complex publics, what debate may or may not achieve and with whom, and what kind of communicative practices and spaces it is necessary to build at critical distance from the 'mainstream' in public culture. Similarly, everyday media cultures do not stand still, and a continuous source of normative and political reflection is folded around the question as to what constitutes meaningful engagement in a system oriented to the incessant production of discursive interaction. Rather, the purpose of this book is to challenge the pervasive idea that it is anti-racist refusal which is fracturing publics and silencing speech. Freedom of speech, as it is currently understood in practices of media balance, ideologies of open debate and demands for a unitary public, functions as a structure of racialized coercion. The idea of 'free speech' is being used to discipline expression, demand conformity, and reanimate racist discourses as markers of free thinking and expression. If anything constitutes the voluble silencing so regularly diagnosed in contemporary culture, it is this.

1 This complexity extends to the variations of and internal tensions within liberal thought on freedom of speech. An adequate engagement with this is simply beyond the scope of this book, but that should not be taken as evidence of a desire to promote a simplistic and reductive characterization. My focus in the chapter's analysis is on those arguments that are most frequently reproduced in public discourse, which most thoroughly neglect questions of power and social structure, and which are thus most vulnerable to advancing the postracial presumption under discussion.

2 As Alan Haworth argues, in his reading of *On Liberty*, Mill's emphasis on 'the liberty of thought and discussion' is not merely an element of the defence of free speech, it is the foundational priority (1998: 24–6). This perhaps explains why it is so often treated as a transhistorical given regardless of political and communicative conditions; see for example, Brian Winston: 'Reason is fed by information, freely communicated. To abridge that freedom is to strike at reason' (2012: xiii).

3 This is a pronounced tendency, but far from an uncontested one within liberal thought. The work of Jeremy Waldron on the 'harm in hate speech', for example, has underlined the ways in which acts of hate speech corrode a 'public good of inclusiveness', constituting an 'environmental threat to social peace' in providing legitimation for acts of discrimination, while acting cumulatively on their targets, where the message is

'don't be fooled into thinking you are welcome here. The society around you may seem hospitable and non-discriminatory, but the truth is that you are not wanted' (2012: 2). For a further discussion of Waldron see Titley (2019: 141–50), and for a very useful overview of debates about hate speech, freedom of speech and theories of speech and communication, see Maitra and McGowan (2012). This latter book also provides a good introduction to Critical Race Theory's influential engagement with the social harm and consequences of racist speech, which for reasons of argument flow I have not attempted to introduce in this chapter. For an authoritative overview, see Delgado and Stefancic (2012).

4 This can also be illustrated by noting the banal extent to which the converse holds. Colin Kaepernick's 'taking the knee' during the playing of the national anthem at NFL games in the US was punished for offending the nation, not celebrated as a telling instance of the national commitment to freedom of expression. The Irish football player James McClean has been regularly pilloried in the British popular press for refusing to wear a Remembrance Day poppy – and thus offending the nation's 'war dead' – rather than held up as exercising the 'freedoms they died to defend', and so forth.

Abernathy, G. (2019) 'Trump is not a racist. His voters aren't either', *The Washington Post*, 7 August, available at: https://www.washingtonpost.com/opinions/2019/08/07/trump-is-not-racist-his-voters-arent-either (last accessed 7 September 2019).

Adams, R. (2019) 'UK's Prevent strategy "biggest threat to free speech on campus"', *The Guardian*, 27 June, available at: https://www.theguardian.com/uk-news/2019/jun/27/uks-prevent-strategy-biggest-threat-to-free-speech-on-campus (last accessed 7 September 2019).

Adut, A. (2018) *Reign of Appearances: The Misery and Splendor of the Public Sphere*. New York: Cambridge University Press.

Ahmed, S. (2009) 'Liberal multicultualism is the hegemony – it's an empirical fact: a response to Slavoj Žižek', *LibCom*, available at: http://tiny.cc/wdfpkz (last accessed 1 March 2020).

Ahmed, S. (2010) 'Feminist killjoys (and other wilful subjects)', *The Scholar and Feminist Online*, 8(3).

Alexander, C. (2017) 'Racing Islamophobia', in F. Elahi and O. Khan (eds), *Islamophobia: Still a Challenge for Us All*. London: Runnymede Trust, pp. 13–15.

Appel, J. (2019) 'Revolutionary quotes from centrist history', McSweeney's Internet Tendency, available at: https://www.mcsweeneys.net/articles/revolutionary-quotes-from-centrist-history (last accessed 1 March 2020).

Back, L., Sinha S. and Bryan, C. (2012) 'New hierarchies of belonging', *European Journal of Cultural Studies*, 15(2): 139–54.

References

Balibar, E. and Wallerstein, I. (1991) *Race, Nation, Class: Ambiguous Identities*. London: Verso.

Barker, M. (1981) *The New Racism: Conservatives and the Ideology of the Tribe*. London: Junction Books.

Battaglia, A. (2006) 'A fighting creed: the free speech narrative in the Danish Cartoon Controversy', *Free Speech Yearbook*, 43(1): 20–34.

Bittner, J. (2019) 'Is there freedom of speech in Germany?', *The New York Times*, 1 October.

Bleich, E. (2011) *The Freedom to be Racist?* New York: Oxford University Press.

Bond, C., Mukandi, B. and Coghill, S. (2018) '"You cunts can do as you like": the obscenity and absurdity of free speech to Blackfullas', *Continuum: Journal of Media and Cultural Studies*, 32(4): 415–28.

Boochani, B. (2018) *No Friend but the Mountains: The True Story of an Illegally Imprisoned Refugee*. Tr. O. Tifighian. London: Picador.

Boulila, S. (2019) *Race in Post-Racial Europe: An Intersectional Analysis*. London and New York: Rowman & Littlefield.

Braidotti, R. (2013) *The Posthuman*. Cambridge: Polity.

Bray, M. (2017) *AntiFa: The Anti-Fascist Handbook*. London: Melville House.

Brown, K. E. and Saeed, T. (2015) 'Radicalization and counter-radicalization at British universities: Muslim encounters and alternatives', *Ethnic and Racial Studies*, 38(11): 1952–68.

Brown, W. (2018) 'Neoliberalism's Frankenstein: authoritarian freedom in twenty-first century "democracies"', *Critical Times*, 1(1): 60–79.

Busby, E. (2018) 'Claims students have created university free speech crisis have been "exaggerated"', *The Independent*, 27 March.

Butler, J. (1998) 'Merely cultural', *New Left Review*, 227: 33–43.

Camp, J. T., Heatherton, C. and Karuka, M. (2019) 'A response to Nancy Fraser', *Politics/Letters*, 15 May, available at http://quarterly.

politicsslashletters.org/a-response-to-nancy-fraser (last accessed 1 March 2020).

Camus, J. Y. and Lebourg, N. (2017) *Far-Right Politics in Europe*. Tr. J. M. Todd. Cambridge, MA: Belknap.

Carey, J. (1992) *Communication as Culture: Essays on Media and Society*. New York and London: Routledge.

Clover, J. (2017) 'Free speech year', *Los Angeles Review of Books*, 21 September, available at: https://blog.lareviewofbooks.org/essays/free-speech-year (last accessed 1 March 2020).

Cooper, D. (2013) 'Question everything? Rape law/free speech', *Critical Legal Thinking* [online], 28 November, available at http://criticallegalthinking.com/2013/11/28/question-everything-rape-law-free-speech (last accessed 25 November 2018).

Davies, W. (2018) 'The free speech panic: how the right concocted a crisis', *The Guardian*, 26 July, available at https://www.theguardian.com/news/2018/jul/26/the-free-speech-panic-censorship-how-the-right-concocted-a-crisis (last accessed 17 August 2019).

Dean, J. (2009) *Democracy and Other Neoliberal Fantasies*. Durham, NC: Duke University Press.

Delgado, R. and Stefancic, J. (2012) *Critical Race Theory: An Introduction*, 2nd edn. New York: New York University Press.

de Noronha, L. (2018) 'Race, class and Brexit: thinking from detention', *Verso Blog*, available at: https://www.versobooks.com/blogs/3675-race-class-and-brexit-thinking-from-detention (last accessed 1 March 2020).

de Noronha, L. (2019) 'Deportation, racism and multi-status Britain: immigration control and the production of race in the present', *Ethnic and Racial Studies*, 42(14): 2413–30.

Dobbernak, J. (2014) 'Sovereignty, security and muscular liberalism: debating "Sharia courts" in Britain', *EUI Working Paper* RSCAS 2014/103.

References

Eddo-Lodge, R. (2017) *Why I'm No Longer Talking to White People about Race*. London, Bloomsbury.

El-Tayeb, F. (2011) *European Others: Queering Ethnicity in Postnational Europe*. Minneapolis: University of Minnesota Press.

Essed, P. and Muhr, S. L. (2018) 'Entitlement racism and its intersections: an interview with Philomena Essed, social justice scholar', *Ephemera: Theory and Politics in Organization*, available at www.ephemerajournal.org/contribution/entitlement-racism-and-its-intersections-interview-philomena-essed-social-justice (last accessed 17 February 2020).

Fenton, N. (2016) *Digital, Political, Radical*. Cambridge: Polity.

Ferree, M. M., Gamson, W. A., Gerhards, J. and Rucht, D. (2002) 'Four models of the public sphere in modern democracies', *Theory and Society* 31: 289–324.

Finney, N. and Simpson, L. (2009) *Sleepwalking to Segregation? Challenging Myths about Race and Migration*. Bristol: Policy Press.

Fredrickson, G. M. (2002) *Racism: A Short History*. Princeton: Princeton University Press.

Freeden, M. (2008) 'European liberalisms: an essay in comparative political thought', *European Journal of Political Theory*, 7(1): 9–30.

Freedman, D. (2017) 'Media power and the framing of the *Charlie Hebdo* attacks', in G. Titley, D. Freedman, G. Khiabany and A. Mondon (eds), *After Charlie Hebdo: Terror, Racism and Free Speech*. London: Zed Books, pp. 209–22.

Froio, C. (2018) 'A new nativism or a new racism? French far-right and Islam', *Reset Dialogues on Civilization*, 10 November, available at: https://www.resetdoc.org/story/froio-new-nativism-o-new-racism-french-far-right-islam-2015 (last accessed 1 March 2020).

Gayle, D. (2018) 'Thousands march in "free speech" protest led by right-wing figures', *The Guardian*, 6 May.

Gelber, K. (2017) 'Using free speech as a weapon', *Policy Forum*, available at: https://www.policyforum.net/using-free-speech-weapon (last accessed 1 March 2020).

Gelber, K. (2019) 'Norms, institutions and freedom of speech in the US, the UK and Australia', *Journal of Public Policy* [online], 25 June, available at https://www.cambridge.org/core/journals/journal-of-public-policy/article/norms-institutions-and-freedom-of-speech-in-the-us-the-uk-and-australia/9A5B4540C9EECEEE50CB6C32F97FC321 (last accessed 17 February 2020).

Gelber, K. and Brison, S. J. (2019) 'Digital dualism and the "speech as thought" paradox', in S. J. Brison and K. Gelber (eds), *Free Speech in the Internet Age*. New York: Oxford University Press, pp. 12–32.

Gillespie, N. (2018) 'Debate: the message of anti-racism has become as harmful a force in American life as racism itself', *Reason Magazine*, available at: https://reason.com/2018/11/09/the-message-of-anti-racism-has-become-as (last accessed 1 March 2020).

Goldberg, D. T. (2015) *Are We All Postracial Yet?* Cambridge: Polity.

Göle, N. (2017) *Daily Lives of Muslims: Islam and Public Confrontation in Contemporary Europe*. London: Zed Books.

Goodhart, D. (2014) 'Racism: less is more', *The Political Quarterly*, 85(3): 251–8.

Goodhart, D. (2017) 'White self-interest is not the same thing as racism', *The Financial Times*, 2 March, available at: https://www.ft.com/content/220090e0-efc1-11e6-ba01-119a44939bb6?mhq5j=e1 (last accessed 3 March 2020).

Gray, H. (2017) 'Race', in L. Ouellette and J. Gray (eds), *Keywords for Media Studies*. New York: New York University Press, pp. 161–5.

Gregory, D. (2004) *The Colonial Present*. Oxford: Blackwell.

Guénolé, T. (2015) 'Attentats à Paris: non, Alain Juppé, les Français musulmans n'ont pas à se justifier', *L'Obs*, 17 November, available at: http://leplus.nouvelobs.com/contribution/1450166-attentats-a-paris-non-alain-juppe-les-francais-musulmans-n-ont-pas-a-se-justifier.html (last accessed 1 March 2020).

References

Hage, G. (2017a) *Is Racism an Environmental Threat? Debating Race.* Cambridge: Polity.

Hage, G. (2017b) 'Not afraid', in G. Titley, D. Freedman, G. Khiabany and A. Mondon (eds), *After Charlie Hebdo: Terror, Racism and Free Speech.* London: Zed Books, pp. 259–61.

Hajjat, A. (2017) 'A double-bind situation? The depoliticization of violence and the politics of compensation', in G. Titley, D. Freedman, G. Khiabany and A. Mondon (eds), *After Charlie Hebdo: Terror, Racism and Free Speech.* London: Zed Books, pp. 79–94.

Haworth, A. (1998) *Free Speech.* London and New York: Routledge.

Haworth, I. G. (2019) 'Trump and the flawed definition of racism', *The Times of Israel,* 31 July, available at: https://blogs.timesofisrael. com/trump-and-the-flawed-definition-of-racism (last accessed 1 March 2020).

Hervik, P. (2011) *The Annoying Difference: The Emergence of Danish Neonationalism, Neoracism and Populism in the Post-1989 World.* New York: Berghahn Books.

Hesse, B. (2004) 'Im/plausible deniability: racism's conceptual double bind', *Social Identities,* 10(1): 9–29.

Husband, C. and Alam, Y. (2011) *Social Cohesion and Counter-Terrorism: A Policy Contradiction?* Bristol: Policy Press.

Jungherr, A., Posegga, O. and An, J. (2019) 'Discursive power in contemporary media systems: a comparative framework', *The International Journal of Press/Politics* [online], https://journals. sagepub.com/doi/full/10.1177/1940161219841543 (last accessed 17 February 2020).

Kamola, I. (2019) 'Dear Administrators: to protect your faculty from right-wing attacks, follow the money', *AAUP Journal of Academic Freedom,* 10.

Kassem, R. (2016) 'France's real state of emergency', *New York Times,* 4 August.

References

Kaufmann, E. (2017) '"Racial self-interest" is not racism: ethno-demographic interests and the immigration debate', *Policy Exchange*, March.

Klein, A. (2012) 'Slipping racism into the mainstream: a theory of information laundering', *Communication Theory*, 22: 427–48.

Kumar, D. (2012) *Islamophobia and the Politics of Empire*. Chicago, IL: Haymarket.

Kundnani, A. (2014) *The Muslims Are Coming! Islamophobia, Extremism and the Domestic War on Terror*. London: Verso.

Langton, R. (2018) 'Blocking as counter-speech', in D. Fogal, D. Harris and M. Moss (eds), *New Work on Speech Acts*. Oxford: Oxford University Press, pp. 144–64.

Lennard, N. (2019) *Being Numerous: Essays on Non-Fascist Life*. London: Verso.

Lentin, A. (2016) 'The lure of "frozen" racism', *Occupied Times* [online], 31 March, available at https://theoccupiedtimes. org/?p=14225 (last accessed 18 November 2018).

Lentin, A. (2018) 'Beyond denial: "not racism" as racist violence', *Continuum: Journal of Media & Cultural Studies*, 32(4): 400–14.

Lentin, A. and Titley, G. (2011) *The Crises of Multiculturalism: Racism in a Neoliberal Age*. London: Zed Books.

Lister, R., et al. (2015) 'PREVENT will have a chilling effect on open debate, free speech and political dissent', *The Independent*, 10 July.

Maitra, I. and McGowan, M. K. (2012) *Speech and Harm: Controversies over Free Speech*. Oxford: Oxford University Press.

Mammone, A., Godin, E. and Jenkins, B. (eds) (2013) *Varieties of Right-Wing Extremism,* London: Routledge.

Marlière, P. (2015) 'Charlie Hebdo and the dawn of French McCarthyism', *Open Democracy*, 17 August, https://www. opendemocracy.net/en/can-europe-make-it/charlie-hebdo-and-dawn-of-french-mccarthyism/ (last accessed 1 March 2020).

Meech, D. (2019) 'Auckland University refuses to remove white supremacist signs from campus', *The Spinoff*, available at: https://thespinoff.co.nz/society/30-09-2019/auckland-university-wont-remove-white-supremacist-signs-from-campus (last accessed 1 March 2020).

Meer, N. and Mouritsen, P. (2009) 'Political cultures compared: the Muhammed cartoons in the Danish and British press', *Ethnicities*, 9(3): 334–60.

Meng, M. (2015) 'Silences about Sarrazin's racism in contemporary Germany', *The Journal of Modern History*, 87(1): 102–35.

Mills, C. W. (2017) *Black rights/white wrongs: The critique of racial liberalism*. New York and Oxford: Oxford University Press.

Mitropoulos, A. (2017) 'Consequentialism and the protection of fascist entitlement', *S0metim3s*, available at: https://s0metim3s.com/2017/08/15/free-speech-and-consequences (last accessed 1 March 2020).

Mondal, A. A. (2018) 'The shape of free speech: rethinking liberal free speech theory', *Continuum: Journal of Media and Cultural Studies*, 32: 4 503–17.

Mondon, A. and Winter, A. (2017) '*Charlie Hebdo*, Republican secularism and Islamophobia', in G. Titley, D. Freedman, G. Khiabany and A. Mondon (eds), *After Charlie Hebdo: Terror, Racism and Free Speech*. London: Zed Books, pp. 31–45.

Morsi, Y. (2017) *Radical Skin, Moderate Masks*. London: Rowman & Littlefield.

Moskowitz, P. E. (2019) *The Case Against Free Speech: The First Amendment, Fascism, and the Future of Dissent*. New York: Bold Type Books.

Mottram, R. (2008) 'Protecting the citizen in the twenty-first century: issues and challenges', in P. Hennessy (ed.), *The New Protective State: Government, Intelligence and Terrorism*. London: Bloomsbury, pp. 42–65.

Mouritsen, P., Faas, D., Meer N. and de Witte, N. (2019) '*Leitkultur* debates as civic integration in North-Western Europe: the nationalism of "values" and "good citizenship"', *Ethnicities*, 19(4): 632–53.

Murji, K. and Solomos, J. (eds) (2015) *Theories of Race and Ethnicity: Contemporary Debates and Perspectives*. Cambridge: Cambridge University Press.

Myklebust, J. P. (2019) 'Holocaust experts: don't let deniers talk on campus', *University World News*, 6 April, available at: https://www.universityworldnews.com/post.php?story=20190405151913839 (last accessed 1 March 2020).

Nadi, S. (2017) 'The ideology of the Holy Republic as part of the colonial counter-revolution', in G. Titley, D. Freedman, G. Khiabany and A. Mondon (eds), *After Charlie Hebdo: Terror, Racism and Free Speech*. London: Zed Books, pp. 291–303.

Ongün, E. (2019) 'No, we don't have the "right to be Islamophobic"', *Jacobin*, 9 October, available at https://www.jacobinmag.com/2019/09/france-insoumise-islamophobia-racism-melenchon-pena-ruiz (last accessed 15 January 2020).

Peters, J. D. (2005) *Courting the Abyss: Free Speech and the Liberal Tradition*. Chicago, IL: University of Chicago Press.

Peters, J. D. (2008) 'Afterword: in quest of even better heresies', in A. Phillips, R. Kunelius and E. Eide (eds), *Transnational Media Events: The Mohammed Cartoons and the Imagined Clash of Civilizations*. Gothenburg: Nordicom, pp. 275–88.

Philips, W. and Milner, R. (2017) *The Ambivalent Internet: Mischief, Oddity, and Antagonism Online*. Cambridge: Polity.

Pigott, S. (2017) 'Anti-Muslim activists, white nationalists and anti-government figures join Pam Geller in NYC to protest Linda Sarsour', Southern Poverty Law Centre *Hate Watch*, 26 May, available at: https://www.splcenter.org/hatewatch/2017/05/26/anti-muslim-activists-white-nationalists-and-anti-government-figures-join-pam-geller-nyc (last accessed 1 March 2020).

References

Pitcher, B. (2009) *The Politics of Multiculturalism: Race and Racism in Contemporary Britain*. Basingstoke: Palgrave Macmillan.

Plenel, E. (2016) *For the Muslims*. London: Verso.

Post, R. (2013) *Democracy, Expertise, Academic Freedom: A First Amendment Jurisprudence for the Modern State*. New Haven: Yale University Press.

Povenelli, E. A. (2011) *Economies of Abandonment: Social Belonging and Endurance in Late Liberalism*. Durham, NC and London: Duke University Press.

Pyrhönen, N. (2012) *The True Colours of Finnish Welfare Nationalism*. Helsinki: University of Helsinki.

Renton, D. (2019) *The New Authoritarians: Convergence on the Right*. London: Pluto Press.

Riemer, N. (forthcoming) 'Disciplinarity and the boycott', in D. Landy, R. Lentin and C. McCarthy (eds), *Enforcing Silence: Academic Freedom, Palestine and the Criticism of Israel*. London: Zed Books.

Roediger, D. (2008) *How Race Survived US History: From Settlement and Slavery to the Obama Phenomenon*. London: Verso.

Rosenfeld, S. (2019) *Democracy and Truth: A Short History*. Philadelphia: University of Pennsylvania Press.

Rouse, C. M. (2019) 'Liberal bias: the new reverse racism in the Trump era', *American Anthropologist*, 121(91): 172–6.

Rydgren, J. (2005) 'Is extreme right-wing populism contagious? Explaining the emergence of a new party family', *European Journal of Political Research*, 44: 413–37.

Saini, A. (2019) *Superior: The Return of Race Science*. Boston: Beacon Press.

Sankin, A. (2017) 'How activists of color lose battles against Facebook's moderator army', *Reveal News*, 17 August, https://www.revealnews.org/article/how-activists-of-color-lose-battles-against-facebooks-moderator-army (last accessed 15 January 2020).

References

Scott, J. W. (2017) 'On free speech and academic freedom', *AAUP Journal of Academic Freedom*, 8.

Shafik, M. (2018) 'Free speech on campus', The Economist Debates, *The Economist*, 17 April.

Shand-Baptiste, K. (2020) 'We don't need more of the same bigoted debate', *The Independent*, 29 January, available at https://www.independent.co.uk/voices/racism-bbc-question-time-today-times-radio-lbc-broadcast-a9308396.html (last accessed 30 January 2020).

Sharma, S. and Nijjar, J. (2018) 'The racialized surveillant assemblage: Islam and the fear of terrorism', *Popular Communication*, 16(1): 72–85.

Sian, K. (2017) 'Born radicals? Prevent, positivism and "race thinking"', *Palgrave Communications*, 3: 1–8.

Simpson, R. M. and Srinivasan, A. (2018) 'No platforming', in J. Lackey (ed.), *Academic Freedom*. Oxford: Oxford University Press, pp. 186–209.

Sivanandan, A. (1990) *Communities of Resistance: Writing on Black Struggles for Socialism*. London: Verso.

Smith, E. (2020) *No Platform: A History of Anti-Fascism, Universities, and the Limits of Free Speech*. London: Routledge.

Song, M. (2014) 'Challenging a culture of racial equivalence', *British Journal of Sociology* [online], 65(1): 107–29.

Stolcke, V. (1995) 'Talking culture: new boundaries, new rhetorics of exclusion in Europe', *Current Anthropology*, 36(1): 1–24.

Susen, S. (2011) 'Critical notes on Habermas's theory of the public sphere', *Sociological Analysis*, 5(1): 37–62.

Taylor, K.-Y. (2016) *From #BlackLivesMatter to Black Liberation*. Chicago, IL: Haymarket.

Taylor, P. C. (2013) *Race: A Philosophical Introduction*, 2nd edn. Cambridge: Polity.

Titley, G. (2019) *Racism and Media*. London: Sage.

References

Toor, A. (2015) 'France's sweeping surveillance law goes into effect', *The Verge*, 24 July.

Traverso, E. (2019) *The New Faces of Fascism*. London: Verso.

Turner, C. (2018) 'Universities which "no platform" controversial speakers will face government intervention', *The Telegraph*, 3 May.

Turner, J. (2018) 'Internal colonisation: the intimate circulations of empire, race and liberal government', *European Journal of International Relations*, 24(4): 765–90.

Tyrer, D. (2012) 'Race, offence and democracy', *MnM Working Paper* no. 8.

Valluvan, S. (2016) 'What is "post-race" and what does it reveal about contemporary racisms?', *Ethnic and Racial Studies*, 39(13): 2241–51.

Valluvan, S. (2019) *The Clamour of Nationalism*. Manchester: Manchester University Press.

Vigoreaux, E. (2016) 'Pour poursuivre la soeur d'Adama Traoré, la maire veut faire payer la commune', *L'Obs*, 16 November, available at: https://www.nouvelobs.com/justice/20161116.OBS1315/pour-poursuivre-la-s-ur-d-adama-traore-la-maire-veut-faire-payer-la-commune.html (last accessed 1 March 2020).

Virdee, S. (2014) *Racism, Class and the Racialized Outsider*. London: Macmillan.

Volkmer, I. (2014) *The Global Public Sphere*. Cambridge: Polity.

Wade, P. (2015) 'Racism and liberalism: the dynamics of inclusion and exclusion', *Ethnic and Racial Studies*, 38(8): 1292–7.

Waldron, J. (2012) *The Harm in Hate Speech*. Boston, MA: Harvard University Press.

Waklker, T. (2018) *Channel 4 News*, 25 April, available at: https://www.youtube.com/watch?v=1_6APlOR_jg (last accessed 3 March 2020).

Weber, C. (2015) *Queer International Relations*. New York: Oxford University Press.

References

Wekker, G. (2016) *White Innocence: Paradoxes of Colonialism and Race*. Durham, NC and London: Duke University Press.

Winston, B. (2012) *A Right to Offend*. London: Bloomsbury.

Wodak, R. (2015) *The Politics of Fear: What Right-Wing Populist Discourses Mean*. London: Sage.

Wolfe, P. (2016) *Traces of History: Elementary Structures of Race*. London: Verso.

Zeroula, F. (2016) 'Cinq mois après la mort d'Adama Traoré, le "deuil n'est pas fait" à Beaumont-sur-Oise', *Mediapart*, 27 December, available at: https://www.mediapart.fr/journal/france/271216/cinq-mois-apres-la-mort-d-adama-traore-le-deuil-n-est-pas-fait-beaumont-sur-oise?onglet=full (last accessed 1 March 2020).

academic freedom 124–6
Ahmed, Sara 49
Alt-Right 118–19
anti-fascism 127–9
anti-Muslim racism 23, 59, 63–5, 67–8, 72–96, 101–3
anti-racism as censorship 8, 24, 57–60, 111–12
apartheid in South Africa 6, 17

Barati, Reza 70
Barker, Martin 106–7
blackface controversies 114
Blair, Tony 73
Bleich, Eric 2
Brexit 30, 40, 50, 107
Bond, Chelsea 69
Boochani, Behrouz 69–70
border politics and migration 41–5, 69–70, 102
Boycott, Divestment, Sanctions (BDS) strategy 119
Brown, Wendy 112–14
Butler, Judith 135

Charlie Hebdo attacks, aftermath 62–5, 91–4, 98–9
Clover, Joshua 120
communication, theories of 34–6, 130–1

consequentialism 33–6, 38, 57, 121
contrarianism 10, 56–61, 133
Cooper, Davina 34
counter-speech 122–7, 131
Critical Race Theory 139

Danish cartoons crisis 89–94
Davies, William 9
de Noronha, Luke 42–6
désolidarisation 81, 95
Dobbernak, Jan 84–5

Eddo-Lodge, Reni 47–50, 55–6, 127
El-Tayeb, Fatima 28
English Defence League 110
Essed, Philomena 114

far-right actors and discourse 100–3, 109–12
fascism 17, 105–7, 115, 127–8
First Amendment (USA) 74, 105, 118, 121, 125
Freeden, Michael 32
Froio, Caterina 102

Gelber, Katharine 9, 66, 73
Goldberg, David T. 27
Goodhart, David 7, 40, 46

Index

Gray, Herman 54

Hage, Ghassan 92
Hajjat, Abdellali 81
hate speech 2, 123–4, 138–9
Haworth, Alan 13, 35
Hervik, Peter 89–90
Hesse, Barnor 17, 37
hijab debates 87–8
Hollande, François 63–4

immigration scepticism 109–10
integration politics in Europe
    67–8, 82–95
intellectual dark web 125
Islamophobia 93–4

Juppé, Alain 82

Kassem, Ramzi 62
Kaufmann, Eric 40, 46
Kundnani, Arun 75–6

Langton, Rae 131
late liberalism 83–6
Lentin, A. 19, 37–8
liberal theories of free speech 12,
    14, 32–6, 48–9

Mandela, Nelson 3–4
marketplace of ideas 4, 38, 118,
    119, 121, 125
Marlière, Philippe 64
McSweeney's Internet Tendency
    3–6
Meng, Michael 58
Middlebury College, Charles
    Murray controversies 129
Mitropoulos, Angela 127

Mondal, Anshuman A. 14–15, 31
Morsi, Yassir 95–6
multiculturalism 83–6

nationalism
    and governmentality 86–90
    and neoliberalism 112–14
networked media environment
    20–1, 35, 50–4, 131–2,
    135–6
Nijjar, Jasbinder 80–1
no platforming 127–30

Obama, Barack 28
On Liberty (Mills) 35, 138
Operation Nexus 44

pedagogy of offence 93–5
Peters, John Durham 104, 116,
    121
political correctness 10, 111–12,
    133
populism 112–15
postracialism 17–18, 27–9
Povinelli, Elizabeth 83–4
Prevent Agenda 76–80

race as technique of power 44–5
racism
    culturalism 104–10
    denial 19–20, 24, 49–50
    historicity 15–20
    as ideology 4–6, 43–5
    as irrationality 37–8, 46
    scientific theories 17–18, 57–9,
        106, 125
radicalization 75–81
Rasmussen, Anders Fogh 91
Reason magazine 8

Index

Renton, David 101
right to offend 90–5
'Robinson, Tommy' 110
Rose, Flemming 92
Rosenfeld, Sophia 32–4
Rossignol, Laurence 88
Rouse, Carolyn Moxley 57–8

Scott, Joan W. 118
secular universalism in France 29,
    63–5, 85
Shand-Baptiste, Kuba 50
Sharma, Sanjay 80–1
Sivanandan, Ambalavaner 6
Smith, Evan 127–8
Song, Miri 50–1
Spencer, Richard 118, 120, 128
Stop the Islamization of America 103
surveillance and securitarianism
    74–81

Taylor, Paul C. 5, 15, 18
Traoré, Adama and Assa 70–1
Traverso, Enzo 100
True Finns party 98, 108–12
Trump, Donald 20, 39, 100

universities and free speech 7,
    78–80, 117–30

Valluvan, Sivamohan 24
viewpoint diversity 57–8, 118,
    125
Volkmer, Ingrid 54

Walker, Tom 31–3, 39–41, 47–8
'war on terror' 65–6, 72–80, 101
Wilders, Geert 99, 117
Windrush scandal 41–2
Wolfe, Patrick 43